Caroline Wickham-Jones lives in Orkney, and is a Lecturer in Archaeology at the University of Aberdeen. She has worked extensively on Orcadian archaeology for many years, and her current research investigates the impact of the changing landscape of Orkney on the early population of the archipelago.

NORTH
RONALDSAY

PAPA
WESTRAY

Pierowall

WESTRAY

Kettletoft

ROUSAY

EDAY

EGILSAY

Whitehall

WYRE

Birsay

MAINLAND

Balfour

SHAPINSAY

Finstown

Kirkwall

Stromness

St Marys

Rackwick

FLOTTA

BURRAY

St Margarets Hope

SOUTH RONALDSAY

SOUTH WALLS

Burwick

Orkney

A HISTORICAL GUIDE

Caroline Wickham-Jones

BIRLINN

This edition published in 2015 by
Birlinn Limited
West Newington House
10 Newington Road
Edinburgh EH9 1QS

First published in 1998 by
Birlinn Limited, Edinburgh

www.birlinn.co.uk

ISBN 978 1 78027 264 1

British Library Cataloguing-in-Publication Data
A catalogue record for this book is available from the British Library

Typeset by Mark Blackadder

Printed and bound by Grafica Veneta
www.graficaveneta.com

For Guille,

*who has been with me throughout
the writing of this book*

Rubbing from Maeshowe

Contents

List of Illustrations

All illustrations credited RCAHMS are Crown Copyright: Royal Commission on the Ancient and Historical Monuments of Scotland.

All illustrations credited Davidson & Henshall are by kind permission of J.L. Davidson and A.S. Henshall, *The Chambered Cairns of Orkney* (Edinburgh University Press 1989).

All illustrations credited MacGibbon & Ross are taken from David MacGibbon and Thomas Ross, *The Ecclesiastical Architecture of Scotland* (facsmile edition, The Mercat Press 1991).

All illustrations credited MacGibbon & Ross ii are taken from David MacGibbon and Thomas Ross, *The Castellated and Domestic Architecture of Scotland* (The Mercat Press 1991).

List of Plates

Acknowledgements

Many people have helped with the writing of this book. First and foremost I should like to thank all those people in Orkney who, over many years, have provided facilities, advice, friendship and encouragement for my various trips, whether I was working for others, carrying out my own research, or on holiday. A great debt is owed to Ann Brundle and Daphne Lorimer in particular – they have always been most welcoming and helpful, and took on the mega-task of reading through, and commenting on, a version of the completed text. Sally Foster was also very helpful in reading and advising on various chapters, and Heather James of Glasgow University Archaeological Research Division advised over the excavations at Skaill House. All of these people have helped to straighten out various misconceptions, errors and omissions as well as tightening and considerably improving the final message. The staff of the National Monuments Record of Scotland in Edinburgh, in particular Iain Fraser, were very helpful in my quest for plans and should be thanked for all their time and advice. Orkney Islands Council Planning Department in Kirkwall helped with missing site references. Needless to say, any errors that remain are the fault of the author. Since publication of the first edition I have benefited greatly from the expertise of many people in Orkney: thanks to all who have helped.

Finally, my grandmother, though she died long before I was born, introduced me to Orkney by collecting postcards when she was stationed there in the First World War. The collection was a source of fascination during my childhood and I have it by me still.

Illustrations

Every effort has been made to trace the copyright holders and we apologise in advance for any unintentional omissions. We would be pleased to insert the appropriate acknowledgment in any subsequent edition of this publication.

Addresses and Websites

The following organisations and websites will be able to provide further information on any aspects of archaeology and history, in Orkney or beyond.

Orkneyjar
http://orkneyjar.com
Sigurd Towrie's encyclopaedic website covers all you might want to know about archaeology in Orkney and a lot more besides.

Orkney Archaeology Society
PO Box 6213, Kirkwall KW15 1YD
http://orkneyarchaeologysociety.org.uk
Check here if you are planning a trip to Orkney for information about forthcoming lectures as well as news of excavation dates and volunteering opportunities.

Historic Scotland
Longmore House, Salisbury Place, Edinburgh EH9 1SH
Telephone: 0131 668 8600
www.historic-scotland.gov.uk
Historic Scotland provides on-line information about the World Heritage Sites, including various information sheets and other documents.

The Orkney Museum
Tankerness House, Broad Street, Kirkwall KW15 1DH
Telephone: 01865 873535
http://www.orkney.com/museums

Visit Orkney
The Travel Centre, West Castle Street,
Kirkwall KW15 1GU
Telephone: 01856 872856
http://www.visitorkney.com

Orkney Heritage Society
PO Box 6220, Kirkwall KW15 9AD
http://www.orkneycommunities.co.uk/ohs

Archaeology Scotland
Suite 1a, Stuart House, Eskmills, Station Road,
Musselburgh EH21 7PB
Telephone: 0845 872 3333
http://www.archaeologyscotland.org.uk

**Royal Commission on the Ancient and Historical
Monuments of Scotland** (RCAHMS)
John Sinclair House, 16 Bernard Terrace, Edinburgh EH8 9NX
Telephone: 0131 662 1456
www.rcahms.gov.uk
*Canmore, the search engine of the Royal Commission on the Ancient
and Historical Monuments of Scotland, holds detailed information
about all recorded sites in Orkney.*

The Orkney Sites and Monuments Record, a local archive of sites,
is available at http://www.library.uhi.ac.uk/smr/orksmr.php

Preface

This book is designed to provide information for those who visit Orkney and would like to know more about its history and how the developments of the past are reflected by the monuments that survive today. As I do not believe that archaeology ever stops (we are now creating the archaeological sites of tomorrow), this new edition tries to bring the story reasonably up-to-date, taking into account both new discoveries and advances in archaeological thinking.

In the space available it is not possible to provide more than a gloss of Orkney's fascinating history, but there is a reading list at the end for those who would like to follow up particular themes in more detail. In addition, Historic Scotland, Orkney Islands Council and others regularly bring out information leaflets and guidebooks on particular sites and periods and these are generally available in the islands and from centralised information centres. Regular visitors to Orkney will also find a visit to the Orkney Room in Kirkwall Library very rewarding.

The Orkney Countryside Code

Please always use stiles and gates to cross fences and walls. Always close gates after you.

Always ask permission before entering agricultural land.

Please keep to paths, and take particular care to avoid fields of grass and other crops.

Do not disturb livestock. In particular cows with calves can be dangerous. Always keep your dog under control, preferably on a lead, and obey 'no dogs' signs.

Please take your litter away with you, and do not light fires.

Please do not pollute watercourses or supplies.

Never disturb nesting birds, and if you do accidentally, please leave the vicinity immediately as there are predators about!

Do not pick wild flowers, or dig up plants.

Please drive with due care and attention – Orkney is a busy place, and not everyone wants to go at 10 mph!

Please exercise consideration when parking – do not obstruct drive-ways, field access, or side roads. Please park off main roads and do not leave your vehicle where it might cause danger to others.

Always take care near cliffs – particularly with children – cliff edges can be crumbly, slidey and dangerous, especially in bad weather.

Walkers should take adequate clothes, and wear suitable footwear as well as telling someone of their plans.

Above all please respect the life of the countryside.

from Tait, C., *The Orkney Guide Book*

Visiting the Sites

The sites chosen for inclusion in the gazetteer have been selected on the basis that they are reasonably easy of access and provide something interesting to see. Many are open to the public, mainly through the agencies of Historic Scotland (HS), and Orkney Islands Council (OIC), but others remain in private hands and many may still be lived in or used as active farms. Visitors should therefore respect the privacy of those who live in, or use, certain sites. Don't assume that you are free to prowl around or photograph every old house – no matter how interesting it is!

There are, of course, a multitude of sites from all periods across Orkney. Many are marked on Ordnance Survey maps, though this does not necessarily mean that they are easy to find, or recognise and understand once you get there. Others are recorded in specialist archaeological and historical literature, and more are found every year. The Orkney Island Archaeologist and Orkney Museum in Kirkwall provide invaluable sources of information about Orkney's archaeological and historical record (addresses are given on page xiv). If you are particularly keen to visit a certain property or site, Visit Orkney in Kirkwall will be able to advise you whether or not it is open. They will also be able to provide information on ferry times and travel arrangements to those islands not served by a regular boat. In addition, new sites are frequently added to the list of monuments with public access, and new trails are laid out for those with an interest in the heritage. The Tourist Office will be able to let you know of any recent additions and provide relevant information. Large groups should always be notified in advance to the correct authority.

Most sites are within easy reach of the road or a footpath. If you have to cross farmland, or open countryside, it is important to follow the Orkney Countryside Code (see page xxiii). The Scottish Outdoor Access Code relies on responsible actions and the recognition that the countryside is used by many. In addition, the weather in Orkney can be both unpredictable and extreme: if you are going to be doing some outside exploring it is advisable to take both warm and waterproof clothing (the wind is often the worst problem), as well as sun cream (the northern latitude means that sunlight is fierce). A torch is useful, especially for the chambered tombs, but also for many of the other sites.

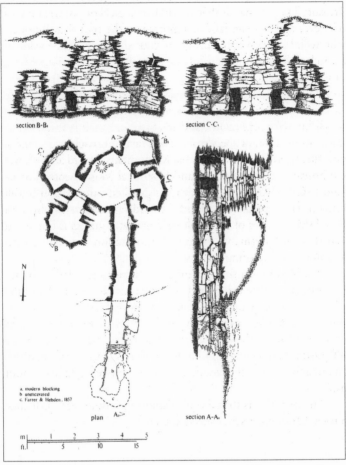

Figure I. The Neolithic tomb at Vinquoy provides a good idea of the excellent preservation of many archaeological sites across Orkney.

When you reach a site it is important to treat it with respect, whether it is in state, local or private ownership, and whether it has been formally consolidated and laid out or not. Stonework should not be disturbed, and nothing should ever be removed from an archaeological or historic site. Very occasionally, a visitor may see something new that appears to be of archaeological interest: finds should be left in place and reported to the Island Archaeologist or Orkney Museum as soon as possible. In Scotland, the law of Treasure Trove demands that any archaeological or historic find (of whatever age or material), be reported to the proper authorities, who will decide on the appropriate course of action. The value of an archaeological find depends very much on the possibility for a proper examination of its find-spot by a professional archaeologist, and the bodies noted above will be happy to advise on this.

In Orkney, the Island Archaeologist has up-to-date information on all known monuments, and may be consulted if you wish to know more about a specific location, or think you have found a new site. In addition, the National Monuments Record at the Royal Commission on the Ancient and Historical Monuments of Scotland (RCAHMS) in Edinburgh has detailed information for all known sites across Scotland, including Orkney. Through RCAHMS a series of archaeological lists and guides is published and these are invaluable sources of information for anyone with an interest in exploring the past.

If this sounds a little daunting, it is not intended to be so. Unfortunately, people have not always respected the remains of the past, but our enjoyment of them, and our children's enjoyment of them, is dependent on all who visit a site: they should leave it as they found it for the generations who follow. Rather than being off-putting, I hope that this book will help to encourage people to go out and discover the wealth of historical interest that lies around us.

The map sheets to use while exploring Orkney are Ordnance Survey Landranger series sheets 5, 6 and 7.

Orkney Isles: Neolithic sites

1. Skara Brae
2. Barnhouse
3. Knap of Howar
4. Links of Noltland
5. Stones of Stenness
6. Ring of Brodgar
7. Ness of Brodgar
8. Ring of Bookan
9. Watch Stone
10. Stane O'Quoybune
11. Stone of Setter
12. Mor Stane

13. Maeshowe
14. Unstan
15. Cuween Hill Cairn
16. Wideford Hill Cairn
17. Quanterness
18. Head of Work
19. Isbister
20. Banks
21. Dwarfie Stane
22. Taversoe Tuick
23. Blackhammer
24. Knowe of Yarso

25. Midhowe
26. Vinquoy
27. Calf of Eday Long Cairn
28. Calf of Eday, North-West
29. Calf of Eday, South-East
30. Quoyness
31. Lamb Ness
32. Point of Cott
33. Holm of Papa Westray South
34. Holm of Papa Westray North

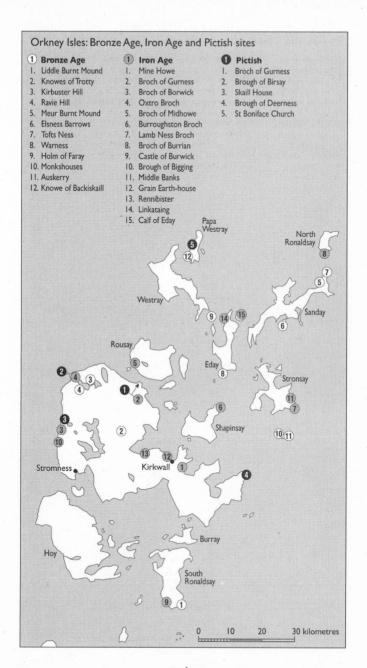

Orkney Isles: Bronze Age, Iron Age and Pictish sites

Bronze Age
1. Liddle Burnt Mound
2. Knowes of Trotty
3. Kirbuster Hill
4. Ravie Hill
5. Meur Burnt Mound
6. Elsness Barrows
7. Tofts Ness
8. Warness
9. Holm of Faray
10. Monkshouses
11. Auskerry
12. Knowe of Backiskaill

Iron Age
1. Mine Howe
2. Broch of Gurness
3. Broch of Borwick
4. Oxtro Broch
5. Broch of Midhowe
6. Burroughston Broch
7. Lamb Ness Broch
8. Broch of Burrian
9. Castle of Burwick
10. Brough of Bigging
11. Middle Banks
12. Grain Earth-house
13. Rennibister
14. Linkataing
15. Calf of Eday

Pictish
1. Broch of Gurness
2. Brough of Birsay
3. Skaill House
4. Brough of Deerness
5. St Boniface Church

Papa Westray

North Ronaldsay

Westray

Sanday

Rousay

Eday

Stronsay

Shapinsay

Kirkwall

Stromness

Burray

Hoy

South Ronaldsay

0   10   20   30 kilometres

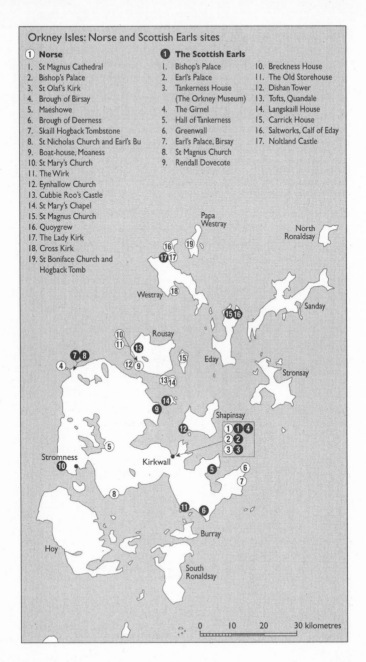

Orkney Isles: Norse and Scottish Earls sites

① Norse

1. St Magnus Cathedral
2. Bishop's Palace
3. St Olaf's Kirk
4. Brough of Birsay
5. Maeshowe
6. Brough of Deerness
7. Skaill Hogback Tombstone
8. St Nicholas Church and Earl's Bu
9. Boat-house, Moaness
10. St Mary's Church
11. The Wirk
12. Eynhallow Church
13. Cubbie Roo's Castle
14. St Mary's Chapel
15. St Magnus Church
16. Quoygrew
17. The Lady Kirk
18. Cross Kirk
19. St Boniface Church and Hogback Tomb

● The Scottish Earls

1. Bishop's Palace
2. Earl's Palace
3. Tankerness House (The Orkney Museum)
4. The Girnel
5. Hall of Tankerness
6. Greenwall
7. Earl's Palace, Birsay
8. St Magnus Church
9. Rendall Dovecote
10. Breckness House
11. The Old Storehouse
12. Dishan Tower
13. Tofts, Quandale
14. Langskaill House
15. Carrick House
16. Saltworks, Calf of Eday
17. Noltland Castle

Papa Westray

North Ronaldsay

Westray

Sanday

Rousay

Eday

Stronsay

Shapinsay

Stromness

Kirkwall

Burray

Hoy

South Ronaldsay

0   10   20   30 kilometres

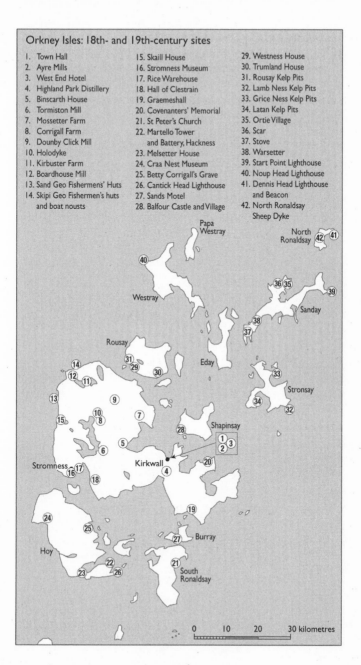

Orkney Isles: 18th- and 19th-century sites

1. Town Hall
2. Ayre Mills
3. West End Hotel
4. Highland Park Distillery
5. Binscarth House
6. Tormiston Mill
7. Mossetter Farm
8. Corrigall Farm
9. Dounby Click Mill
10. Holodyke
11. Kirbuster Farm
12. Boardhouse Mill
13. Sand Geo Fishermens' Huts
14. Skipi Geo Fishermen's huts and boat nousts

15. Skaill House
16. Stromness Museum
17. Rice Warehouse
18. Hall of Clestrain
19. Graemeshall
20. Covenanters' Memorial
21. St Peter's Church
22. Martello Tower and Battery, Hackness
23. Melsetter House
24. Craa Nest Museum
25. Betty Corrigall's Grave
26. Cantick Head Lighthouse
27. Sands Motel
28. Balfour Castle and Village

29. Westness House
30. Trumland House
31. Rousay Kelp Pits
32. Lamb Ness Kelp Pits
33. Grice Ness Kelp Pits
34. Latan Kelp Pits
35. Ortie Village
36. Scar
37. Stove
38. Warsetter
39. Start Point Lighthouse
40. Noup Head Lighthouse
41. Dennis Head Lighthouse and Beacon
42. North Ronaldsay Sheep Dyke

Orkney Isles: 20th-century sites

1. Hatston Airfield
2. Merkister Hotel
3. Twatt Airfield
4. Kitchener Memorial
5. Betty's Reading Room
6. Ness Battery
7. Pier Arts Centre
8. Happy Valley
9. Finstown Boat-house
10. Netherbutton
11. Churchill Barriers
12. Italian Chapel
13. Balfour Battery and Lighthouse
14. Buchanan Battery
15. Flotta Oil Terminal
16. Lyness Pumping Station
17. Wee Fea Communications Centre
18. Garrison Theatre, Hoy
19. Wreck of German Destroyer, Lopness
20. Lettan Radar Station and other remains
21. Bird Observatory

Introduction

Orkney comprises a group of some sixty-seven islands lying off the north coast of Scotland. Today they are easy to reach, by car, train, ferry and plane, though the journey can be long and expensive and some southerners tend to think of them as lying at the edge of 'civilisation'. This was also true in the past: in 1883 John Tudor wrote of their apparent geographical isolation in his guidebook to the islands, and even further back, about 330 BC, the Greek traveller Pytheas of Marseilles claimed that from Orkney one could see the edge of the world.

Nevertheless, throughout the ages Orkney has also lain at the heart of things: for the Norse earls and seafarers who left their Norwegian homeland to settle there, Orkney was a central base from which they could voyage and trade with both the Hebrides and Ireland as well as keeping up with events in Scandinavia and further afield in Europe. Similarly, for those who live in Orkney today, there is little sense of isolation or lack of facilities.

We do not know how Orkney's first settlers viewed their island home, but we do know that Orkney has been inhabited for nigh on 10,000 years. For much of that time the sea has provided the main highway and viewed in this light the waters around Orkney, though treacherous, are also inviting. Rather like a six-lane motorway today, you have to know what you are doing, but the northern seas could lead you directly to your destination and provide varied benefits in the form of sheltered harbours and plentiful supplies.

Any visitor to Orkney today will quickly realise that the modern image of a peaceful cultural backwater has to be dispelled. The islands are certainly peaceful, but agriculture and commerce prosper, and there is industry: from oil processing to whisky distilling, as well as a thriving cultural life and a rich heritage of archaeological remains and natural sites. All of these things combine to form 'the Orkney Experience'.

This 'experience' is quite unique; it is formed from a subtle mix of past events and present conditions. Countless generations of past Orcadians and their visitors have combined to leave their mark on both land and society and it is this contribution that is considered in this guide. It has been said that the key to the present lies through an understanding of the past, and it is hoped that those who use this guide will find that it not only provides information on some of the wonderful archaeological and historic monuments that may be visited in Orkney, but also helps to explain them and their contribution to the islands today.

In 1999 the archaeology of Orkney received the ultimate accolade when the Neolithic sites of Skara Brae, Maeshowe, the Stones of Stenness and the Ring of Brodgar were designated as a World Heritage Site under the title The Heart of Neolithic Orkney. World Heritage status is carefully controlled by the International Council on Monuments and Sites and it is not accorded lightly. It brings benefits but also responsibilities. It is a true reflection of the extraordinary nature of these sites. Since then enhanced investigation has revealed even more about the lives of the Neolithic inhabitants of Orkney through the discovery of remarkable sites, such as Ness of Brodgar, and unique finds, like the Links of Noltland figurine. At the same time, excavation of sites from other periods, such as the Cairns broch or the Viking settlements at Deerness and Snusgar, confirms that the wealth of Orkney archaeology is by no means confined to the Neolithic remains. Whether you are starting your archaeological journey or a confirmed traveller, Orkney is an exciting place to visit.

The Natural Background

Although people are influential in shaping the land, the land is also influential in shaping people, and this is nowhere more important than Orkney where particular features such as the easily shaped stone and the low-lying fertile soils have played a vital role over the millennia. It is therefore necessary to understand a little of the natural history of the islands before we launch into their human history.

Geology and Geomorphology

Most of Orkney is formed of sandstone, laid down in the sea about 380 million years ago. These sandstones differ slightly in type and colour, but collectively they are known as the Old Red Sandstones. They are not particularly hard rocks, and generally split easily into regular slabs, known as flagstones. One curious feature of the sandstones is that in many places they contain large numbers of fossilised fish.

In a few areas, notably around Stromness, remnants of the preceding rocks may be found. These comprise mainly granites and gneisses and geologists suggest that they formed a range of small hilly islands before they were buried by the sediments that would become the sandstones.

Finally, in the island of Hoy there is evidence for volcanic activity that is more recent than the sandstones. There are lava flows in five places in Hoy, though geologists are uncertain whether these are remnants of one large flow or several smaller events. The most famous lava outcrop is at the Old Man of Hoy, where a sandstone stack sits on a hard base of lava that has resisted erosion by the sea.

More recently, though still in the far-off past to humans, the rocks of Orkney have been shaped by the pressure of ice that passed over them during the Ice Age. The last onslaught of ice only disappeared some 10,000 years ago, though this was only the most recent of a series of glaciations stretching back many thousands of years. Orkney would have been covered by many metres of ice and it had a severe effect on the landscape. First of all, as the ice gradually moved across the countryside, it scraped and scoured the land to erode away the surface. Secondly, as it finally slowed down and melted, the scraped-up stones, gravel and soils were dropped to form deposits known as boulder clay, or till.

Thus the landscape has been both reduced and enhanced by the glaciers. Across most of Orkney, it is the till deposits that are most obvious – in some places they are many metres thick and include stones moved by the ice from several miles away. In other places, particularly on the higher hills of Hoy, bare surfaces of scraped rock and steep U-shaped valleys show where the glaciers scoured things out as they passed.

Since the Ice Age, erosion has not, of course, stopped. It is continued in the work of the wind, rain and sea. Of these the sea is perhaps the most active, and in some places severe winter storms cut back the coastline by as much as a few metres every decade. The coasts of Orkney have changed dramatically over the last 10,000 years, but this is also due to a delayed effect of the ice.

During the Ice Age sea levels fell as water was drawn up into the great glaciers that covered the land. At the same time, the land itself sank as it was pressed down by the weight of ice. The net result in Orkney is calculated to have been a drop of more than 30 metres in sea level at the height of the glaciation 15,000 years ago. After the ice melted, water was released back into the oceans, but the land also rose, relieved of the great pressure. As a result sea levels first rose and then fell again and this is a process that is still taking place today, albeit in a less dramatic fashion.

Orkney, therefore, has not always had the familiar outline of today. The first settlers after the Ice Age would have seen larger land masses, of which today's islands are only the inland hills. Those who first visited Orkney found one large island, best accessible through the sheltered waters of Scapa Flow that opened directly from the Pentland Firth to the south. Gradually, through the Mesolithic and Neolithic, rising sea levels flooded the coastal lands and led to the breakup of the archipelago into the island group that we know today. Recent research indicates that sea level only reached present heights about 4,500 years ago, towards the end of the Neolithic. This has obvious implications when we are looking for early sites: much of the land, and the sites which stood on it, has now disappeared. Where sheltered conditions exist, the shallow waters between the current islands may well preserve a unique archaeological record and this is the subject of current research. Even during the Neolithic, some 5,000 years ago, there was more land so that, excitingly, the submerged footprint may include stone-built sites as well as the more ephemeral Mesolithic remains. Gradually the islands have assumed their present shape, but it is clear that even this is not stable. Sea levels are still rising very gradually. What sort of land will the inhabitants of the future know?

The geology of Orkney may seem comparatively simple, but it has left a rich legacy for her settlers. Various minerals occur throughout the islands, and have been worked at different times in the past. These include copper, lead and iron ore. Today, the controversy over the extraction of uranium from south-west Mainland crops up from time to time. Less controversial, but equally contemporary, the exploitation of petroleum from the nearby North Sea bed has had a major impact on recent Orcadian culture. Most recently, the quest for renewable energy has reached Orkney in the form of wind generation on land and the development of marine renewables in the high-energy waters around the islands.

In addition to the mineral wealth, the more common rocks have also helped to shape the past. The sandstone flags split naturally into regular rectangular blocks that make for easy building. Over the millennia, this has been a particular boon to a region without timber for its houses. While the archaeological record has preserved the remains of timber buildings from early in Prehistory, the records show that throughout most of the human past the people of Orkney have had to look elsewhere for building materials. The Neolithic farmers were skilled builders in dry-stone flags, using them for both houses and tombs, as well as for many of the furnishings that would have been made of wood elsewhere in Britain. This means that the archaeological record is more complete than in many other parts of Britain because of the use of more durable materials. Later on, the flagstones were still important for both grand and humble dwellings. Invariably, it is the grander buildings that tend to survive through history, but Orkney has a rich architectural heritage that includes a variety of structures, all of which are well worth exploring.

Landscape and Settlement

To the untutored eye the Orcadian landscape may appear bland. Gentle hills clad with moorland rise above lowland fields. Trees are noticeable only by their absence. But to see only this image is to miss the point: the many riches and subtleties of the topography, vegetation and colouring.

The island coastline provides a dramatic variety of vista, from some of Britain's highest sea cliffs at St John's Head in Hoy – over 330 metres high – to sweeping sandy bays. There are grassy spits, barely linking one rocky headland to another, and deep sea geos, wave-filled cuts into the rocky cliff line. Inland low green farmlands extend, broken by stretches of clear blue water from Orkney's many lochs, both fresh and salt. There are still occasional patches of poorly drained marshland, and above this rise the heather-clad hills, perhaps more majestic for the very roundedness of the terrain. This is not all, however, for in Orkney, as nowhere else, the sky (and associated weather) must also be counted into the order of things. Thus there is forever a changing backdrop which, whether cloud-scape or blue, day or night, adds a dimension usually unnoticed elsewhere.

The islands are accessible and fertile. Transport, both by land and water, is not difficult. Access to the sea is relatively easy, through sheltered bays and harbours to provide a safe anchorage, and clear (if not always well-made) routes over land.

This has been important: it meant, for example, that settlement could spread out. Although islands that once held people are now abandoned, and the density and spread of population has certainly changed, for much of the past it is likely that the general pattern of settlement was not much different from that of today. Small gatherings of dwellings, hardly to be judged as villages by modern standards, lay amid a spread of individual, but not isolated, steadings that might, at various times, reach more, or less, into the hills. Dominating all, the towns: today the burgh of Kirkwall to the east is the county town, while Stromness to the west has lost some of its past trading glory, but it still remains as an important link to the outside world. In between lies Finstown, though Finstown started life relatively recently as a watering hole (more exactly a pub) at one of Orkney's major crossroads.

With people came names. The placenames of Orkney provide a strong reflection of its past, though with each successive overlay the earlier picture becomes more and more faint. Thus, although there is a rich pattern of Norse names, we do not know how the early farmers referred to their settlements at Skara Brae or Barnhouse, or to the monuments that they raised at Maeshowe or Ness of Brodgar. Similarly, the original names have been forgotten for the great broch towers raised in the Iron Age at Gurness and Midhowe. Hints of prehistoric names may indeed be lurking in some nomenclature, but so far they have not been traced.

The name 'Orkney' itself has been traced to the Picts. It was in use by *c.* AD 561, when Saint Columba was concerned for the safety of his missionaries who were working in the north. The old Irish historians referred to the islands as *Insi Orc*, meaning 'the islands of the tribe of the wild boar'. The boar was a well-recognised Pictish totem, and the name was well enough established to be translated and used in Latin, and later on in Norse. In contrast to this antiquity, the name of the main island, 'Mainland', seems surprisingly modern. It stretches back at least to Norse times, however, when it appeared as *Meginland*, 'main island', but other names have also been used. Another Norse name for Mainland Orkney was *Hrossey*, 'island of horses', and it is sometimes referred to as *Pomona*, though Marwick (in *Orkney Farm Names*) has shown that this last name derives from a misreading of a medieval manuscript that was actually noting the fertility of the land.

Pictish names are scarce in the islands, but there is a web of Norse names and these provide a rich source of information. They give detail on how the land was settled and used, on important landmarks for sea-going craft, on local administration systems and taxes, and on the people as they went about their daily business. Placename study is a detailed and serious topic, and this book is not the place for an academic discussion of all the placenames of

Orkney, but it is an interesting topic and there are good works of reference on the subject (e.g. Marwick, H., *Orkney Farm Names,* and Nicolaisen, W. F. H., *Scottish Place-names*). Individual locations of interest are noted in the various chapters.

Vegetation and Climate

Orkney has been farmed for at least 5,000 years, and the present land cover owes much to human interference. Nevertheless, there are still many areas where a more 'natural' vegetation thrives. The coastlands include both herb-rich cliff tops, with a spectacular cover of sea-pinks in early summer, and low-lying lagoons interspersed with rocky shore-lands. Inland, there are poorly-drained marshlands, lowland heaths and intensively tended agricultural lands, both arable and pasture. Higher up lie heather-covered moorlands, although only a few places are high, or exposed, enough for more specialised mountain flora to flourish. Peat is widespread, although it did not begin to form until about 3,000 years ago, long after the first settlers arrived, and since that time it has been extensively harvested.

Not surprisingly, with such a variety of habitat Orkney has a diverse vegetation. Woodlands are rare today, and with one exception (at Berriedale in Hoy) they have been planted in fairly recent times, but there is increasing evidence that this was not always the case. Research on ancient plant remains found in peat bogs indicates that trees were originally more extensive. Although much of the woodland was relatively scrub-like, it included a good variety of species and did not actually disappear until well after the arrival of the first farmers. It is likely that the loss of the woodlands may be explained partly by natural causes, such as a hostile climate, and partly by extended and long-term human interference, as the land was slowly cleared for fields and grazings. Woodland plants tend, therefore, to be missing, but nevertheless the list of Orkney flora is rich and contains many interesting species (see Berry, R. J., *The Natural History of Orkney,* and Bullard, E., *Wildflowers in Orkney*). It even boasts one particularly special plant: *Primula scotica,* the Scottish primrose, which occurs only in the northernmost parts of Scotland and Orkney.

The vegetation is the product of a combination of many factors:

the underlying geology and soils, and human interference are but two of them. Climate is also important. This has been constantly changing since the end of the Ice Age, but it is likely that some factors have remained fairly constant. Wind, for example, is always influential in Orkney, and has played a factor in the present lack of trees. The casual visitor may feel that there is never any shelter from the gale, and indeed high winds do occur throughout the year. Rainfall is not unduly high, however (varying between 1,500 mm average in Hoy and 900 mm in east Mainland), and winters are relatively mild (average 4°C), though summers are rarely very hot (average 12°C). Snow does not generally last long, but summer fogs are frequent. Due to its northern latitude Orkney experiences long summer days when the sun barely sinks below the horizon, but in the winter there is little more than 6 hours daylight. The growth season in Orkney (when the temperature rises above 6°C) lasts between five and six months.

Wildlife

The animals of Orkney are interesting, partly because many that are common in the Scottish mainland are lacking. Foxes and badgers, for example, are not to be found, while hedgehogs and brown hares have both been introduced recently: the hedgehog in the last century; the hare in the nineteenth. Rabbits are common, although they were only introduced into the islands in the twelfth century; both sheep and cattle were introduced by the first farmers 5,000 years ago. One particular breed of sheep is of special interest: the North Ronaldsay sheep, which are particularly small and live almost entirely from seaweed. In North Ronaldsay itself they are kept from the island fields by a circular wall which confines them to the foreshore.

Natural species include otter and seal, as well as a variety of small land mammals. Mice and rats are common, as well as pygmy shrews, but the animal of interest here is the Orkney vole. Orkney voles are a distinct species of vole, quite different from voles in the British mainland, and seem to have been present at least from the time of the early farmers (see Berry, R. J., *The Natural History of Orkney*, p. 127).

The lack of large predators has not only allowed small mammals to flourish, it has also assisted the bird population. Orkney is well known for its abundant and interesting birdlife. The seabirds are perhaps most obvious to the casual visitor, from aggressive Arctic skuas and terns to the colourful, friendly puffins. The varied coastline provides an ideal home for many different species which can be observed with ease. Inland, the farmlands and freshwater lochs provide good habitats for a wide range of species, including curlews and divers, while other species stick to the moorland areas. Finally, encouraged perhaps by the abundance of small mammals as food, there are birds of prey such as golden eagle and hen harrier, as well as kestrel and short-eared owl. In recent years sea-eagles have once again been sighted in the airspace of Orkney and nesting pairs have been reported, a sign of the success of reintroduction programmes further south in Scotland.

Wildlife is not only confined to the land and air – both marine and freshwater animals are also important. The seas around Orkney are rich in fish and shellfish, and have provided an ideal habitat for various fish farms in recent years. On land the freshwater lochs are well known for brown trout, but they and the rivers also provide a home to a variety of invertebrates, including leeches, as well as other fish.

The First Settlers:
Mesolithic Orkney

Evidence for the very earliest (Mesolithic) settlement of Orkney is hazy, and there are no good sites to visit. The first peoples to enter Scotland after the Ice Age were nomadic hunters. They came into Scotland about 9,000 years ago from Ireland and the Continent as the climate improved and trees and plants once more covered the land. We do not know exactly when they crossed to Orkney, but it may have been early because the evidence suggests that Orkney was freed from the weight of ice early on, so that vegetation, in the form of woodlands of birch and hazel trees with open grassy spaces, could develop. Little is known about the animals of Orkney in these times, but on mainland Scotland a diverse fauna is reported. The early Orcadians came over from the mainland in skin boats and dug-out canoes, but they did not settle down. They moved on from time to time, in search of new moorlands for fresh game, or different shorelines for shellfish. Throughout the course of any one year they visited a variety of the separate habitats of Orkney, and they may even have crossed back to the mainland of Scotland at certain times of the year, or every few years.

These hunters left little behind them. They did not build permanent dry-stone houses: they made tent-like dwellings from frames of driftwood or local timber and covered them with skins and other things. These could be moved to the next campsite with relative ease, and only the burnt hearth, or perhaps a circle of boulders from the base of a tent, would be left behind. The hunters used neither metal nor pottery: their tools were made from sharp flaked flint and shaped bone, antler, shell and ivory, while for containers they used wood or skin. Most of these things, along with their clothes and jewellery, have long since disappeared into Scotland's acid soils, and Orkney's earliest settlers are represented only by handfuls of stone flakes.

For this reason their sites can be hard to locate, and their study is a specialised task. But there are other problems as well, and all have hindered our knowledge of Mesolithic Orkney. The considerable changes in sea level that have taken place since the end of the last Ice Age mean that when the early settlers first came to Orkney the sea level would have been much lower. The lands that we now see would have been inland hills to them, and the lowlands and coastlands that they explored must now lie offshore, mainly buried by sand and seawater. An important part of the archaeological record relating to this time lies underwater and has been lost.

On shore, much of Orkney's landscape lies buried under recent sediments, the fertile soils and peat deposits that have developed over the last few millennia. There is little erosion to cut down and reveal the old land surface of 10,000 years ago, so in some instances the traces of the early Orcadians may lie buried well below the present land surface. Only where a plough pulls artefact remains to the surface will they be revealed, and even then it takes the farmer to notice something unusual. This is increasingly difficult as work in the countryside takes place with bigger and bigger machines, and more and more speed. It is surely no accident that some of the best evidence for the early settlement of Orkney was found in the last century, when those walking behind a horse-drawn plough frequently gathered large collections of stone tools from their fields.

Finally, it could be commented that Orkney has attracted many archaeologists over the years, and yet they have apparently uncovered little evidence for the early settlers. This, sadly, seems to reflect archaeological fashion. Up to the 1950s there were several well-known antiquarians, both from Orkney and further afield, who studied and commented on the numerous collections of stone tools from the islands. Some of these collections were recognised as Mesolithic in date. More recently, archaeological theory has concentrated on the analysis of monuments, and their interpretation within the landscape. Orkney has such a profusion of well-preserved sites that it clearly offers great scope for this work, and so the archaeological work here has come to centre round the excavation and interpretation of upstanding remains from periods like the Neolithic. Information about the earliest settlers, who did not construct such remains, was largely neglected, and this fell into agreement with a general pattern of thought that as post-glacial settlement had gradually worked its way north from England through Scotland, so it would arrive last, and relatively recently, in the northern islands. Thus there was a time when many writers argued that Orkney was not settled until the arrival of the first farmers some 5,000 years ago, though we now know that this was not the case.

Nowadays, it is accepted that the pattern of early settlement was not as simple as that, and that there were other influences on the Mesolithic hunters from the west, and north. All this time the Orkney museums and several private collectors have guarded their information: the artefacts themselves. There are several collections of stone tools from Orkney, which include the tiny stone blades and arrowheads known as 'microliths', which were used by these early nomadic settlers.

It can no longer be doubted that Orkney was settled prior to the early farmers, but there is little detail of this settlement. Only recently has research and excavation started to fill in the blanks about this important period of the early history of Orkney.

The nomadic Mesolithic lifestyle means that remains from this period are ephemeral so that this is a hard task, and this is compounded by the changes that have taken place in the landscape since people first arrived in Orkney. Elsewhere in Scotland the evidence indicates that these early settlers often chose to live by the sea and shore from which they could draw all that they needed to live. This means that the lost coastlands of Orkney are key to our understanding of the earliest settlement here. Recent research has tackled the problem of recognising possible underwater remains, but definite sites have still to be found.

For now, a gazetteer of the Mesolithic sites of Orkney is no more than a list of various fields. It does not show the distribution of early settlement, but rather the areas in which archaeologists and others with an interest in such early times have been active and where sites have come to the surface. Nevertheless, two sites have been excavated and provide a little more detail. In the east of Orkney the site of Long Howe comprises a small Bronze Age burial mound from a more recent period. Under the mound, however, archaeologists found traces of Mesolithic remains which had been destroyed during the creation of the burial. The evidence dated to *c.* 6700 BC and probably related to a small hunting camp overlooking a marshy area. More substantial remains were found on the island of Stronsay, where excavation at Links House was able to investigate evidence for a camp comprising several huts or shelters, along with hearths and activity areas. The site at Links House was dated to *c.* 6900 BC, and provided clear evidence of the way in which the early settlers were able to make the most of all that Orkney had to offer.

Links House and Long Howe offer a window on to a long-forgotten world. Other scatters of stone tools indicate that Orkney was not unknown at the time, though population is likely to have been scarce. The interested visitor is better to try to imagine the land, as they travel through it, as it might have been for those who lived here some 10,000 years ago. The first people to arrive in Orkney at the end of the Ice Age found one large island. They must have crossed by boat, probably from the south, into Scapa Flow. Initially, Scapa Flow was a large land-locked bay, entered through a narrow sound with steep cliffs (present-day Hoxa) on either side. Once inside the bay the waters opened to reveal a large body of water offering both shelter and resources and leading into the heart of the island. It must have been a spectacular location, especially for those accustomed to small skin boats or dug-outs. Over time, as sea levels gradually rose, Scapa Flow became more accessible to the sea, but it is a still a dramatic place. Around Orkney, the coastlands extended well beyond the present shore, and a quite different series of lagoons, bays and headlands existed. There was rather more woodland, with stands of birch, hazel and other trees, interspersed with open grassy spaces. The lower lands were marshy and ill drained, while the higher moorlands were not yet peat covered, though they did have heather. The climate was slightly warmer, though it is hard to imagine that the wind did not still make itself felt. In addition to the human settlers there were animals, probably not much different to those of today, though finds of antler suggest that red deer roamed the islands. If so they would have been an important food resource. Other food resources were concentrated around the coast and loch shores. Fish, sea mammals and shellfish were all important to the Mesolithic hunters. Travel around the islands was best undertaken by boat, though sites like Long Howe indicate that people also crossed the interior. We do not know how many people lived in Orkney at this time, and it is important to remember that the Mesolithic lasted for several thousand years: from *c.* 7000 BC to *c.* 4000 BC. Some groups may well have crossed back to the Scottish Mainland at certain times of year, or from time to time, in order to meet up with relatives there, or take advantage of specific resources. One thing that is certain is that these people were well used to a changing world. As sea levels rose, and the land settled from the weight of ice that had covered it, the island archipelago broke up. Nevertheless, people are adaptable and were able to make the most of the plentiful resources that Orkney had to offer.

MESOLITHIC SITES

Mesolithic-type stone tools have been recorded from a number of locations in Orkney. While there are no spectacular sites to visit, Mesolithic material is held by both the Kirkwall and Stromness museums and it is salutary to consider these tiny traces of the past. For those who wish to visit the landscapes where early settlement has been found, Mesolithic tools have been recovered from several of the fields around the loch of Stenness, the lower slopes of Wideford Hill, the fertile fields of Tankerness, and the farmlands of Rendall, all on Mainland. Farther afield, Mesolithic artefacts were recorded below the Neolithic settlement at Knap of Howar in Papa Westray, and at Millfield and Links House in Stronsay.

Early Farmers:
Neolithic Orkney

About 6,000 years ago there were profound changes to the way of life in Scotland. Hunting and gathering gave way to farming as the mainstay of food production. This was probably not a rapid change – it is likely that it took place over a few centuries – but it had far-reaching consequences. The farming people needed a more permanent base in order to tend their crops and look after the animals. Long-term settlements sprang up, and in Orkney the lightweight structures of the Mesolithic nomads were abandoned for well-built structures constructed initially of timber and, later on, of local stone. Furnishings became more elaborate, as did personal goods. Material culture flowered and developed. The tool kit was no longer designed to be easily transported from place to place, so new and fragile materials like pottery could now be incorporated and new methods of design and decoration appear.

As the Neolithic farmers cultivated the land, so nature could, apparently, be controlled and tamed. Permanent settlement and a more assured food supply meant a different outlook on the world and this in turn brought changes to the social order. Individuals could concentrate on the things that they did best so that craft specialists began to arise. People lived and died in the same spot, as had the previous generations, and they started to venerate their ancestors with elaborate monuments that also served as communal markers. These were the pegs that held the people to their territory.

This was only the beginning of a great sweep of change that has accelerated over the last few millennia and arrived (though it has not yet ended) at the complexity of our lives today. From the start, it brought about a completely new series of archaeological sites and other evidence, and this early period, the Neolithic, is particularly well represented in Orkney.

Exactly how the change-over to farming took place in Scotland is still a matter of archaeological debate. The common crops –

primitive forms of barley and wheat – were not native, and neither were sheep and domestic cattle. So, in Orkney, there must have been incomers arriving by boat, probably from neighbouring Caithness and further west. It seems likely that small groups arrived in Orkney with the new ways and the means to set up their new lifestyle. They found a fertile land: as sea levels approached present heights, the archipelago had started to break up, but there were still extensive coastal plains to be taken advantage of, along with gentle valleys leading into the interior. Woodland cover was commonplace, though open stretches of grassland also existed. Nevertheless, the land was already populated. The Mesolithic hunters were not savages and they had a long history of settlement in the islands. They too knew the archipelago; they knew how to get the most out of it and may even have begun to control their own resources by creating clearings or burning woodland to assist the hunting, though always leaving something to regenerate new supplies for the future. Some hunters may have been attracted to the new way of life. It seems likely that many would have taken on the new customs, marrying into incoming families and settling down to look after their domestic stock. At the same time, others may have been more resistant, perhaps maintaining some of the old traditions, even if they were now less important. There is evidence for both hunting and fishing on many Neolithic settlement sites (and, of course, such activities continue to this day). What is interesting is that by *c.* 3800 BC there is no evidence for the Mesolithic way of life in Orkney at all; it has simply disappeared. Is this just a sign of the success of farming? Does it reflect the personal preferences of the time? Or is it perhaps something more sinister – the result of some sort of violence or genocide? At present the evidence is unclear and so it provides scope for some interesting debate among archaeologists. The wholesale scale of this change, the transition from hunter-gatherer to farmer, is also reflected elsewhere across Scotland and the UK.

Neolithic houses

Orkney is unique in that it contains a wealth of evidence of Neolithic settlement. The evidence suggests that the earliest

Neolithic houses were built of timber and excavation is now revealing increasing evidence for these initial dwellings at places like Wideford on Mainland and Braes of Ha'breck in Wyre. Later in the period, however, as timber became scarce, the tradition of building in stone developed. One result of this was the preservation of remarkable detail relating to the Neolithic lifestyle. The quality of Orcadian flagstone meant that it leant itself to sophisticated buildings. In Orkney, houses, and other structures, survive in a better condition than in most of mainland Britain, and some still stand almost to roof height. Study of the timber houses is only just beginning, but initial evidence suggests that they comprised elongated oval dwellings similar to the stone buildings that replaced them.

The best-known Early Neolithic house site so far identified is that at the Knap of Howar in Papa Westray, which it is also possible to visit. Knap of Howar comprises an individual farmstead of two adjoining buildings. Both are long and have rounded ends. They were cut into a pre-existing mound of midden (domestic rubbish, like a compost heap) and the walls are made of local flagstone with a midden core. Here, as elsewhere in the Neolithic, midden was an important building material: people used old, well-rotted midden heaps so that by the time it was used for construction it would not have been smelly, and it provided good insulation as well as adding stability to the dry-stone walls. The larger building at the Knap of Howar is interpreted as the dwelling house and inside there was a stone and timber partition dividing it into two rooms, together with traces of furnishings, again using both stone and timber. Carefully built stone hearths were found in each building. The smaller building was divided into three rooms and has, if anything, more complex fittings including various stone-built shelves and cupboards. It is interpreted as a workshop. Each house has an entrance set into one end, but they are also connected by a passage through the long central wall.

The use of old midden in the construction at the Knap of Howar indicates that this was not the first settlement on the site, but so far there is no trace of any earlier settlement from which the midden rubbish must have built up – it may have been dismantled when the existing structures were built.

Unlike many of the Neolithic settlement sites in Orkney, the

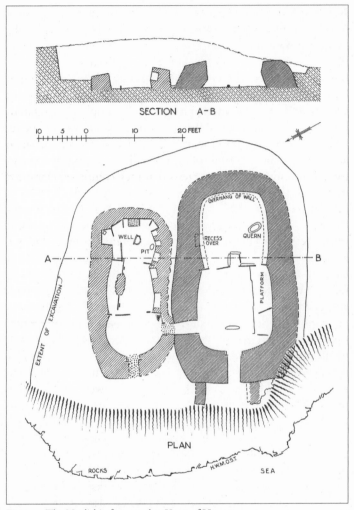

Figure 2. The Neolithic farmstead at Knap of Howar.

house at the Knap of Howar stands alone. Most of the known Neolithic houses are grouped into small villages, though recent finds at Smerquoy near to Finstown suggest that other individual farmsteads existed.

In the later Neolithic period settlement comprised small

villages. Orkney contains the remains of several village sites, some of which have been excavated. Of these, the earliest to be investigated is still the best known – that at Skara Brae, which was originally uncovered by a storm in 1850. The houses at Skara Brae show some similarity with the construction techniques of Knap of Howar, but there is also evidence for development and alteration in building method with time and other evidence suggests that Late Neolithic Orkney was a sophisticated place.

Skara Brae lies at the south end of the Bay of Skaill on the west Mainland coast. There are the remains of at least ten houses, in varying states of preservation. All except one are joined together by a winding covered passage and its offshoots. Like the buildings at Knap of Howar, the Skara Brae houses are built of flagstone set with midden. The village grew and changed over time, and the earlier houses survive as only a few courses of stone. They are roughly circular in plan and comprise one main room with a square, slab-built, central hearth on either side of which the wall was recessed to contain a bed. The door is at one end, and at the other end there is a stone 'dresser'. The later houses are much the same shape as the earlier ones and contain many of the same features, but they are larger and the beds are no longer set into wall recesses; instead they project out towards the hearth. The passage that unites the houses seems to be a late addition, towards the end of the life of the settlement. If you visit the village today, the remains of the early houses can be made out. They are more ruinous than, and generally lower than, the later buildings.

The Skara Brae houses contain all sorts of small fitments and oddities, from which we have been able to reconstruct some of the minutiae of Neolithic life. Beneficial preservation conditions means that the material culture of our Neolithic ancestors is preserved in intimate detail. Saddle-shaped quernstones were often laid at one end of the room, near the dresser, and there were also sunken stone boxes lined with clay to make them watertight. These may have been used for storing and processing food such as shellfish. Various cells were built into the house walls and some may have been used for storage, though several have underfloor drains and it is likely that these served as latrines. The inhabitants used fine decorated pottery, known (to us) as Grooved Ware, and they made jewellery of animal bone. Fragments of preserved rope have been found, together with sharp stone flakes and blades to serve their everyday needs.

Skara Brae, as we see it, is a sophisticated settlement site, with clear evidence that each house was carefully planned and thought out prior to building. Because of this, different archaeologists have put forward their own views of Neolithic life. Were the Neolithic villages highly communal places where everyone lived in harmony? Or were they claustrophobic settlements, where life was closely regulated by social oppression? As with so much academic work, the same evidence may be used to fit many, often opposing, theories, and they probably say more about the different researchers involved, and the society in which they live today, than they do about the past! While personal space may have been regarded very differently at Skara Brae, it was possible to close off each house by barring the door from the inside, and we are reminded by elements such as individual pieces of incised art of the possibility of personalising space through the use of colour and decoration.

As at the Knap of Howar, there is also evidence from Skara Brae of one non-dwelling structure. House 8, set slightly apart, to one end of the village, is built in a similar fashion to the other houses, but there are significant differences and it contains none of the usual furnishings. House 8 is the only free-standing structure at Skara Brae; it was approached through a small porch, and though it contains a central hearth, there is also evidence that processes involving fire took place elsewhere inside. A flue leads out of the building opposite the door and, on either side of it, there are recesses that were found to contain rounded, fire-cracked stones. Round the rest of the building the walls contained many small shelves and alcoves. When House 8 was excavated it was found to contain much debris from the making of stone tools as well as broken fragments of pottery and it has been interpreted as a workshop used, among other things, for pottery and tool making.

There have been several different campaigns of excavation at Skara Brae since its discovery in 1850. It may seem surprising, therefore, that even today not all of the site has been examined. Work has always concentrated on the main settlement area, but there are also Neolithic remains extending away from the site along the dune

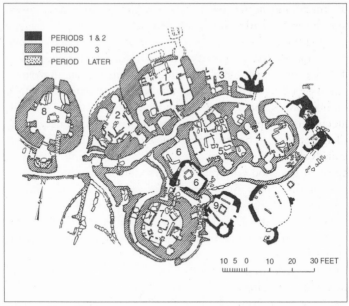

Figure 3. Skara Brae.

faces to either side. In addition, traces of the fields and enclosures that were farmed by Skara Brae's inhabitants have been recorded behind the village.

Other Neolithic settlement sites exist across the Mainland and in the islands and some have been excavated. New sites are also still identified from time to time. Most of these sites have either been covered by recent sediments or partly lost to the sea, with the result that there is little to see except where they are specifically laid out. The site at Barnhouse, on the loch of Harray at Stenness in Mainland, is one such site, laid out for the visitor by Orkney Islands Council. The settlement here is of particular interest because of its proximity to the Standing Stones of Stenness and for the archaeological work that has taken place. The houses at Barnhouse were not as well preserved as those at Skara Brae and the remains that can be seen today are entirely reconstructed according to information gleaned during excavation. The walls stand to only a few courses of stone, but it is possible to see that the buildings followed the same design as the earlier Skara Brae houses, with beds recessed into the walls at either side of the hearth.

Barnhouse offers an interesting contrast to Skara Brae because it was not preserved under a mountain of sand, but rather below the soil in an everyday field. Ploughing and other agricultural activities have taken their toll of the remains so that little remains of the house walls, though archaeological detective work can still shed much light on the life of the village. If there are other Neolithic villages waiting to be discovered below the Orcadian fields then it is likely that they will be in a similar state of preservation to Barnhouse. It is a good example of how exciting new discoveries may be made even today. Skara Brae is an exception for Orcadian, and even British, archaeology, but it is a site that has helped us to add much detail to the picture of daily life in the Neolithic.

Barnhouse may not be as spectacular as Skara Brae, but it is interesting because it also sheds light on a different aspect of the Neolithic settlements in Orkney. As well as the domestic houses, Barnhouse contains other structures. In the portion of the settlement that has been excavated there are two quite different buildings. One is similar to the ordinary houses, but it has two main rooms, both with hearths and 'bed recesses'. The other structure is much larger than the other houses; it sits on a slightly raised platform and was surrounded by a wall, with an elaborate entrance and internal passage. It may have been used for communal gatherings and other rituals. Barnhouse includes a ritual element to go with the domestic side of life. This is not surprising, given its location at the heart of the Stenness complex, and it is clear that each new excavation has much to teach us about Neolithic life.

Domestic life

Several of the Orcadian Neolithic sites lie in shell sands, which means that there has been an unusually rich preservation of the everyday trappings of their occupants. Across most of Scotland the soil is very acid, so that household belongings, like bone pins, awls and jewellery, have long since dissolved away, together with the structures themselves. In Orkney we are lucky because not only do we have the houses and furnishings, built of stone, but also many of the objects that lay around their interiors. This has afforded us a rare glimpse of everyday Neolithic life.

Stone was still important to provide sharp cutting edges and durable scrapers for leather working, as well as new-fangled axes, useful no doubt in clearing ground for crops. These were supplemented with a wide range of bone and antler tools, from fine needles and awls to heavier mattocks and shovels. No doubt there were wooden tools also, as well as handles and hafts, but these have rarely survived. Pottery was common (much of it highly decorated) and fragments of very large as well as small pots have been found, which must have been used for a range of tasks from cooking to the preparation and storage of food and drink.

Evidence from the middens provides information relating to diet. The people of the Neolithic were essentially farmers who grew a limited range of crops, such as oats and barley, and tended cattle, sheep and pigs. They supplemented the produce of their fields from the surrounding land however: there is evidence on several sites for the use of fish as well as shellfish, and on occasion sea mammals, such as seals or whales (perhaps from strandings), would be made use of. Local birds provided an important resource, and both bone and antler attest to the use of deer. Towards the end of the life of the village at Skara Brae these resources may have come into their own as the evidence indicates that the encroaching coast made farming more difficult as salt spray and sand blows affected the fertility of the fields. In time it seems that life at Skara Brae became unsustainable and so the families drifted away in search of more secure land elsewhere.

Neolithic life was not all work: bone dice were found at Skara Brae, as well as a variety of jewellery including different types of bone and shell beads, tusk pendants and decorative bone pins. In addition, a number of small containers of stone and bone with traces of red ochre were found and there were worn lumps of haematite that seem to have been used in much the same way as pencils. Pigment was perhaps used for body paint, as well as to work on clothing or carvings. Some of the more enigmatic finds from Skara Brae include many stones with finely-incised carvings. These are generally thought to be art: they appear abstract to the modern eye and are difficult to interpret, though some have seen landscape views and other images amongst the scratchings.

It is still difficult to interpret the finer details of Neolithic life, but it is clear that there was more to being a Neolithic farmer than the simple struggle for survival.

Ceremony in the Neolithic

Even in the Stone Age life was not confined to the dwelling house and its immediate fields. From all over Britain there is evidence of a complex ceremonial side to the culture at the time, but Orkney is particularly special, not only because of the wealth of remaining ceremonial monuments, but also because of their proximity to other types of Neolithic site. Only rarely do we have the opportunity to look at the way that villages, ceremonial centres and tombs might have interacted together.

The main focus of surviving ceremonial monuments from Neolithic Orkney lies in central Mainland, on the isthmus between the lochs of Stenness and Harray. Here a great complex of monuments was built in the Neolithic, including three henges, two of which also had stone circles, as well as a number of individual standing stones. Henges are circular monuments of earth, comprising a flat central platform with a surrounding ditch and a bank around the outside. Some are large and impressive with wide platforms, deep ditches, and high banks; others are more modest in scale.

The northernmost of the Orkney monuments is the Ring of Bookan, a simple structure of earth, but to the south lie the Ring of Brodgar and the Stones of Stenness, both of which included stone circles on the central platform. In recent years this area has become famous for the excavations at Ness of Brodgar, which have opened our eyes to a completely new type of Neolithic monument. Ness of Brodgar lies to the south of the Ring of Brodgar and was completely unknown until 2002, when a decorated slab was brought to the surface of the field by the plough. Since then, excavation has revealed a complex of monumental structures of a scale previously unimagined for the Neolithic anywhere in the United Kingdom. The detailed interpretation of Ness of Brodgar has yet to be finalised (and it is described in detail below), but already it acts as a reminder of just how limited and biased existing interpre-

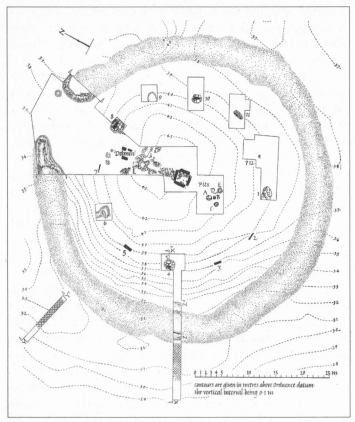

Figure 4. Excavation plan of the Stones of Stenness.

tations of the Neolithic can be. Although sites like the stone circles which occur across the UK had been thought to act as foci for Neolithic ceremony and ritual, it is now possible to interpret them as mere portals indicative of much richer remains in the vicinity; they are important to us because of their survival and visibility, but were perhaps not quite so important in the Neolithic.

Nevertheless, sites like the Stones of Stenness have been the subject of much detailed archaeological research from which a clear picture of the site has emerged so that they are still central to our understanding of Neolithic life. Where henge sites such as this are excavated, it is common to find evidence for the construction of various structures and settings on the interior platform. At the centre of the henge platform at the Stones of Stenness lay a square setting of stone slabs identified as a hearth and around this there were various stone settings and pits as well as settings and slots for timber posts. The activities that took place here clearly demanded a variety of structures, but it is not possible to say exactly how these would have appeared. Only four stones survive today at the Stones of Stenness, but the excavations revealed that there were originally twelve, possibly with others to the centre (where two have since been reconstructed). Radiocarbon dates from material recovered during the excavations indicated that the Stones of Stenness was in use by 3000 BC.

The Ring of Brodgar lies to the north, along the peninsula, and is the largest of the three sites, but it remains a more enigmatic monument. The Ring of Brodgar has not been the subject of detailed excavation across the interior, though the ditch has been investigated. It is estimated that there were originally sixty stones at Brodgar in a circle measuring almost 104 metres across. As at Stenness, the surrounding ditch was cut into the bedrock; it would have been an impressive sight during the life of the monument, with steeply sloping sides and originally over 3 metres deep and 10 metres across. Clearly a vast amount of material was removed to make the ditch, but there is no trace of an outside bank. Estimates have been made of the time needed to build the circles: it stands at 12,500 man-hours for the Stones of Stenness and 80,000 for the Ring of Brodgar. It is unlikely that the small nearby village of Barnhouse would provide all the labour necessary over the years, and so it is generally considered that these must have been central monuments, constructed by, and important to, people from across Orkney. One theory suggests that individual communities brought material from their villages to raise as standing stones, and it is indeed possible to discern distinctions among the stones that survive today.

In addition to these impressive monuments, the complex includes several individual standing stones as well as many tomb sites. Many of the standing stones have since fallen or been deliberately removed and only a few survive today. The best known are the Comet Stone by Brodgar, the Watch Stone by the Stones of

Figure 5. The Ring of Brodgar, from the Rev. Barry's *History*, published in 1805.

Stenness, and the Barnhouse Stone in a field to the south-east. Significant omissions today include the Odin Stone, which once stood in the field to the north of the Stones of Stenness and was of local importance into the early nineteenth century and a partner to the Watch Stone, evidence for which was uncovered during road workings.

Recent research, including geophysical work, field survey and excavation, indicates that much of the land along the peninsula was taken up with monumental structures, including the walled complex at Ness of Brodgar, and it may have extended south as far as Maeshowe. The whole area was, no doubt, a significant place for the inhabitants of Neolithic Orkney. We cannot tell precisely how these different monuments were used, but the area clearly functioned as a unity in which individual elements each had their own role to play, rather as any great cathedral comprises a number of smaller chapels and cross sites, both inside and outside the building. Participation may have been restricted and varied, depending on individual rites. Activity may also have taken place at night. It has been suggested that the Ring of Brodgar, at the heart of the complex, may have functioned as a lunar observatory and this may well be so, but the dates at which it would work best for this apparently lie around 1500 BC, whereas the circle had been built long before that. Nevertheless, astronomical observations, including various constellations as well as the moon, are likely to have been important to the Neolithic farmers.

The neck of land between the lochs was clearly also important in the Neolithic. Others have pointed out the significance of the location (see Ritchie, A., *Prehistoric Orkney*), which lies at the heart of the fertile farmlands, at the meeting point of sky and water, and yet surrounded by low hills. Though sea level would have been a metre or so lower when work on these sites first started, this was still a watery, liminal place. While the loch of Harray was a boggy landscape, the loch of Stenness would have presented open stands of freshwater, merging into dense reed beds towards the edges. Over time, during the life of the monuments, rising sea levels served to isolate the ridge of land that had been chosen for activity, perhaps acting to emphasise the importance of this spot. As the loch of Harray became increasingly waterlogged, so occasional storm surges entered the loch of Stenness, resulting in the gradual salination of the loch. The sea today enters the loch through the shallows at the Brig of Waithe and dates indicate that this was one of the last places in Orkney to be flooded by the sea as sea levels reached present heights around 2500 BC.

There is no other ceremonial complex in Orkney that even approaches the central heartland of the Brodgar Peninsula in size, and no other henge sites have been recognised in the islands, but there are many other standing stone sites. Most stones stand alone today, but this was not necessarily so in the past, and little research has been done to identify any possible timber settings or other structures with which they might originally have been associated. It is unlikely that every stone was used for exactly the same purposes, but their users were linked by a common culture, and this is likely to have involved periodic trips to the great centre in Mainland Orkney. People no doubt gathered here in different groups at different times of the year, and various rituals and ceremonies were carried out. These may well have involved the treatment of the dead, as well as other religious rites and even legal or political decisions.

Today we tend to compartmentalise life into separate boxes: religion, politics, home, but this was not always so in the past. Certainly it is clear that there was some centralised organisation and emerging hierarchy that worked well, if people could get together to plan and build such a large complex, over what was probably a long period of time. It is likely that the different Neolithic villages were in regular contact. Population was increasing, and life had changed considerably from the mobile hunter gatherers of the preceding millennia.

Burial Sites

The rituals at the Neolithic ceremonial sites may well have included rites pertaining to the dead. But where were the dead actually buried? In Orkney we have at least part of the answer. The islands are dotted with burial mounds, some of which relate to Neolithic times, while others are more recent.

The majority of the Neolithic tombs seem to have been built as mounds rising above the fertile fields of their farmlands. There was a central chamber built of stone to house the remains of the dead, and this was covered by a mound of stone or turf. The entrance lay at one end of a stone passage and could be sealed, often with a large stone. There are two distinct types of tomb in Orkney, though as yet the reason for the difference is little understood.

'Maeshowe'-type tombs are only found in Orkney and consist of a long passage that leads to a rectangular central chamber from which small side cells have been built into the walls (e.g. Maeshowe and Cuween in Mainland). 'Orkney–Cromarty' type tombs are more widely distributed elsewhere in Scotland, and in them the passage leads to a chamber which is subdivided by upright flagstones. The subdivisions give the appearance of animal stalls, hence these tombs are commonly known as 'Stalled Cairns' (e.g. Blackhammer and Midhowe in Rousay). Orkney–Cromarty tombs do not have side cells, though there are a few hybrid tombs that combine elements of both designs, such as Unstan in Mainland and Isbister in South Ronaldsay. In general, Stalled Cairns are thought to predate Maeshowe-type tombs.

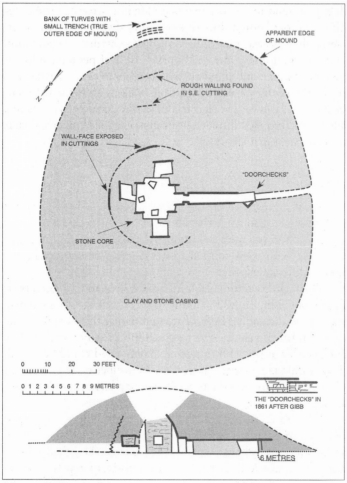

Figure 6. Maeshowe.

There is evidence that some tombs originally contained large quantities of human bone and from this it is generally assumed that bone in similar quantity must have been present in all tombs, though our understanding of the rituals that surrounded the preparation and burial of bodies has been hampered by the fact that many tombs were opened and 'explored' long ago. In fact, few tombs have survived with their contents relatively intact for study by modern excavation so the discovery of a new site is always exciting. Where the records are good enough it is clear that the bones are found in two very different states. While some tombs contained articulated, recognisable skeletons, many others contained large quantities of disarticulated bone (i.e. bones that no longer maintained the shape of the skeleton). Sometimes the disarticulated bones lay piled together into a heap, in other cases they had been carefully separated into different piles with skulls in one part of the tomb, long bones in another, and so on (as at the Knowe of Yarso in Rousay). Some tombs, such as Isbister in South Ronaldsay, contained only a few bones from each of many individuals.

These differences point to both similarities and differences in the burial rites. Some communities placed their dead within the tombs for the bodies to fall apart as the flesh decayed, hence the complete skeletons. Others seem to have kept the body elsewhere while the flesh was decaying. Some may have used excarnation platforms, exposing the dead to carrion feeders, and only gathering up the bones to place them in the tomb once they had been thoroughly cleaned, others may have favoured other processes.

Different communities clearly respected the dead in different ways while the corpse retained a recognisable identity. But they were no less important once the flesh had gone and it may be that the transformation from body to bone was a significant one. In the long term the tombs were regarded as the resting place of the ancestors, though the veneration of those ancestors did not necessarily require that individual skeletons be respected. The shared preservation of bones was enough to maintain the rites, and perhaps general identity, of any single community. Once the flesh had decayed, therefore, the bones could be swept up, in some cases into a central heap, in other cases into distinct piles. Human bones are not the only bones found in the tombs. Many also contained quantities of animal bones and this evidence is interesting because there is some evidence that different tombs may have concentrated on different species. At Isbister, for example, there was evidence for the burial of the complete carcasses of sea-eagles in the tomb, while the Knowe of Yarso contained the bones from at least thirty-six red deer, and Cuween Hill Cairn in Mainland contained twenty-four

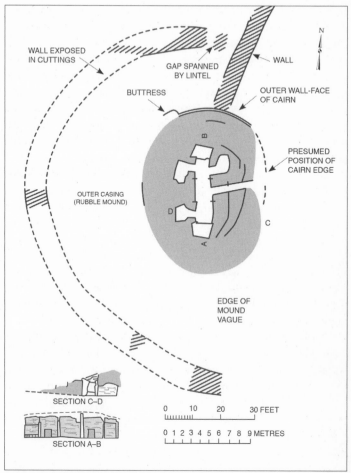

Figure 7. Isbister.

dog skulls. This emphasis on a particular species has led to the suggestion that the animals were totemic and reflect the different identities of the individual communities of Neolithic Orkney. It is a nice idea, but hard to prove!

Alongside the bones, other goods have been found in the tombs, especially flaked stone tools of flint and sherds of pottery. It may be, however, that some of these relate to the activities of the mourners, rather than to actual grave goods. It is impossible to reconstruct the exact rituals with which the dead were laid to rest in the Neolithic, but it is clear that the tombs were long-term monuments. Their construction alone must have required considerable effort (10,000 or more man-hours has been estimated for some monuments), and most seem to have been used again and again. The chambers were carefully built to remain stable and dry, and the management of the remains of the dead was carefully organised and maintained. The tombs were repeatedly entered, and must have been a living part of any community.

It is likely that activity not only took place inside the tomb, but also round the outside. There is little evidence for this, because excavation in the past generally tended to centre on the tomb and chamber, but there are hints. At Pierowall Quarry, in Westray, the excavator interpreted the outer of two revetments to the cairn as 'primarily a façade for display'. Both here and at Quoyness in Sanday the finds recovered outside the tomb (pot sherds and stone tools) suggested that various activities had been taking place away from the chamber. This is supported by evidence from tombs on the Scottish mainland.

Other chambers have direct 'links' to the outside world. At Taversoe Tuick in Rousay there is a tiny 'chamber' outside that connects to the tomb, perhaps to give access to, or communication with, the spirits of the ancestors. At Maeshowe, it was possible to seal the entrance from the inside, but it has been calculated that there would have been a gap at the top of the blocking stone and the suggestion is that this allowed for communication with the spirits within, even when the tomb was closed. Finally, several tombs have engravings that have been interpreted as art. These may be found both inside the chamber (Maeshowe, and the Holm of Papa Westray) and outside the cairn, where they were probably visible to passers-by (the tomb at Pierowall Quarry was destroyed by the quarrying that led to its discovery, but the fine carved slab from its construction may be seen in the Westray Heritage Centre in Pierowall). While we cannot be sure of the precise meaning of art such as this, the strength of the designs suggests that it conveyed a strong meaning.

Neolithic art in Orkney is not confined to burial; it also

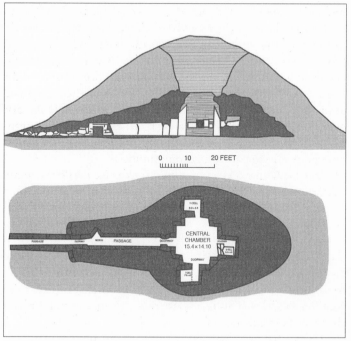

Figure 8. Nineteenth-century drawings of Maeshowe.

occurred on settlement sites, and there are other links between the tombs and the dwelling houses of the time. Archaeologists have made links between the form of the chamber and side cells in a Maeshowe-type tomb which is very similar to the form of the houses at Skara Brae, and the other village sites. Similarly, the form of a Stalled Cairn parallels the design of the houses at the Knap of Howar. These differences are matched by change in the material goods and because of this it is common to formalise the division of Neolithic Orkney into two chronological periods: Early and Late. The Early Neolithic is typified by houses such as that at Knap of Howar, together with the Stalled Cairns, while the inhabitants of Late Neolithic Orkney were more familiar with settlements like Skara Brae and Maeshowe-type tombs.

In the Early Neolithic those who lived at the Knap of Howar used round-bottomed bowls with some linear decoration below the rim (known as Unstan Ware), while at Skara Brae flat-bottomed, grooved bowls (Grooved Ware) were most common. These pottery groupings are also reflected in the style of the pots found in the tombs, but it is hard to be sure of the precise meaning of these differences. What is clear is that the tombs did not function alone, but rather as social elements within the Neolithic landscape.

Some ceremony no doubt took place at the tombs themselves, while other activities were carried out at the great circle sites, and other rituals are likely to have gone on in the settlements. Whether these dealt with the minutiae of life or of death, they went together to make up the fabric of Neolithic society. It is difficult to place that fabric within the wider landscape, but there are some interesting pointers. The physical and possibly calendrical settings of the henges and stone circles has already been touched upon. The importance of the astronomical landscape is reinforced by most tombs, the entrances of which tend to face south-east, into the midwinter sunrise. The great tomb of Maeshowe, on the other hand, faces south-west, directly into the setting midwinter sun. This distinction, it seems, was very deliberately planned. One of the most spectacular archaeological sights of Orkney must be at midwinter, when the sun shines directly down the passage at Maeshowe to strike the back of the chamber. Maeshowe was definitely something special, but all tombs were clearly placed in prominent locations, and some may have been almost tower-like. They were not only celestially sited, but also physically important. It has been pointed out that the tombs were generally set just outside the good agricultural land and it may be that they helped to consolidate the relationship between each small village community and the lands of its ancestors. They would certainly have acted as prominent land markers, particularly in such a gentle landscape as Orkney and this was enhanced by the fact that they housed the bones of previous generations.

The chambered tombs were communal monuments, respecting the ancestors, lands and emblems of Neolithic society. Today they still stand out in the Orkney landscape, and it is notable that far more tombs than settlement sites have been discovered, but this is largely the result of preservation and survival: over the years the stone-built houses have proved far more susceptible to collapse and they have often served as a good source of building stone for later structures, so that many are hidden today. Chambered tombs, on the other hand, held strong mythologies and tended to be respected so that even the modern farmer will rarely drive his plough over the middle of the collapsed heap of stones that marks the site of an ancient burial.

NEOLITHIC SITES (see map, p. xxviii)

1 Skara Brae, Mainland HY 231187

Historic Scotland; signposted; car park; visitor centre; café.

Skara Brae was completely unknown until 1850, when a great storm removed the sand cover from part of the village. Since then the site has been excavated on several occasions and the remains have been consolidated to provide a real glimpse of everyday life in the Stone Age. The village dates back to about 3100 BC, and was in use until about 2500 BC. Only the lower courses of stonework survive in the earlier houses, but the later houses (from about 2800 BC) survive to roof height. Coastal erosion has reduced the size of the settlement as it survives today, but archaeologists do not think that it was ever very much larger. There are six main surviving house structures, overlying the earlier remains, and estimations of the size of the community vary, but it is likely that between 50 and 100 people lived here, in family groups.

Skara Brae was inhabited over a long period of time and of course the different houses and structures underwent much alteration in that time. Nevertheless, the main details of life were remarkably uniform, and remained so throughout the life of the settlement. Inside the houses the stone furnishings – beds, dressers and hearths – may be seen, and the visitor display houses some of the everyday goods, the pottery and stone tools, of the people. One of the main questions for visitors to Skara Brae relates to the roofing materials. Unfortunately nothing survives of the original roofs, but these could have been made of driftwood or of whalebone, which probably supported a thatch of eel grass from local reed beds. It is possible that stone slates were also used in roof construction and evidence for this has been found from the ceremonial site at Ness of Brodgar.

Today, much of the village appears to be semi-subterranean as the houses are linked by passages roofed over with flagstones. This is really an illusion because the houses were not sunk into the ground, but were built as separate structures into pre-existing mounds of midden rubbish and the passages between were only roofed towards the end of the life of the village. This style of building provided both stability and insulation in the harsh northern climate.

To the west of the main settlement lies a building that is separated from and slightly different to the other structures. This is interpreted as a workshop: it is entered through a lobby and contained many recesses and two hearth areas, and inside there was much debris from the manufacture of pottery and stone tools. Altogether the construction of the settlement was a sophisticated process, incorporating drains and lavatories set into some of the inter-mural cells, as well as being carefully laid out to ensure the privacy of each family. Life for the people of Skara Brae was not without its comforts.

It is likely that in clement weather the inhabitants of Skara Brae were an outdoor people, carrying out many of their daily tasks on the surface of the midden which surrounded their houses and in the fields round about. They kept cattle, sheep or goats, and pigs, and they grew barley and wheat. In addition, they fished, collected shellfish, and hunted seabirds and mammals as well as red deer. At the time of settlement, the sea lay further off and there was a salty lagoon between the village and the sea, separated from the sea by a line of sand dunes. This would have been a landscape with plentiful resources for the inhabitants of Skara Brae.

The people of Skara Brae had a rich material culture including finely decorated pottery, sharp stone blades, and carefully made bone tools. They made jewellery of bone and shell, and gaming pieces have been recognised amongst the artefacts from the site. In addition some of the slabs from which the houses and passages are built have been decorated with incised designs of diamond and triangle shapes. There is a small museum on site and artefacts from the village may also be seen in The Orkney Museum in Kirkwall, and in the National Museums of Scotland in Edinburgh.

2 Barnhouse, Mainland   HY 307127

OIC; signposted walk from the Stones of Stenness; small car park at the Stones.

The first building at the village of Barnhouse took place about 3200 BC and the site was inhabited until about 2900 BC. Today, only the lower courses of stonework are visible, and the village as presented is completely reconstructed according to the results of excavation in the 1980s. Nevertheless, it is possible to see the remains of several Skara Brae-like houses here. Excavation revealed traces of at least thirteen houses, though it is not known whether all were occupied at the same time. Like the earlier houses at Skara Brae, they have beds recessed into the walls, and they all have central hearths and well-built stone drains.

Two of the structures are quite different from the others. One is a big, double-roomed structure. The other is also a larger building, of the same rounded shape as the others, but with a massive outer wall, a monumental entrance, and slightly different features inside. It seems likely that this building was designed for communal activity, perhaps related to the activities going on at the Stones of Stenness nearby; the central hearth of this structure has been linked to that lying at the centre of the stone circle. The settlement at Barnhouse dates to the same time as the Stones of Stenness and it is not difficult to imagine the people from the village using, and perhaps even looking after, the impressive standing-stone monument close by.

Barnhouse is interesting because it lies at the heart of a Neolithic landscape that includes such a variety of other monuments: the Stones of Stenness, the Ring of Brodgar, Ness of Brodgar, and Maeshowe tomb are all visible from the settlement, as well as a number of smaller sites.

3 The Knap of Howar, Papa Westray   HY 483518

Historic Scotland; signposted.

The farmstead at the Knap of Howar was built about 3500 BC and continued in use for about 500 years. It comprises two buildings, built side-by-side and interlinked by a cross passage. The larger of the buildings seems to have been the dwelling house; it is divided into two rooms with a central hearth in the inner room and various furnishings. The doorway lies at the inner end of a short passage, and still retains the holes for the checks by which it could be barred. The smaller building could be reached down a further short passage in one of the long walls – interestingly the door lay at the far end of this passage. This smaller building could also be entered directly from the outside and it is generally interpreted as a workshop; it is divided into three rooms and also had a hearth and the traces of various fittings. As at Skara Brae, there is no sign of the original roofs for the structures, which may have been of thatch based on timber or whalebone supports.

The inhabitants of the Knap of Howar were farmers with crops as well as animals, and they also hunted and fished. At the time of occupation, the sea lay further away from the settlement and it is possible that Papa Westray was linked to neighbouring Westray by a sandy spit.

The farmstead at Knap of Howar is one of the earliest stone-built dwellings in Britain, and it provides a puzzle: the buildings stand on a layer of pre-existing midden refuse, so there must have been an earlier settlement very close by. No trace of this has yet been found. Was it destroyed by the builders of the houses that survive today when they designed their modern, up-to-date dwelling? Or does it lie still buried, awaiting discovery?

4 Links of Noltland, Westray
HY 428493

Signposted; small car park; footpath across beach.

Neolithic remains at the Links of Noltland were recorded by Petrie in the nineteenth century, but the dunes here are mobile and the site then disappeared from view until archaeological work to redis-cover it was carried out in the 1970s. The site comprises a substantial Neolithic settlement, together with the remains of later, Bronze Age houses. The Neolithic houses are similar in design to those of Skara Brae with beds projecting towards a central hearth and other furnishings such as dressers. They are free-standing and cover a considerable area under the modern dunes. The walls are double-skinned and bound with midden as at Skara Brae, and one building, Structure 9, is notable because within the cavity of the walls lay thirty cattle skulls. Although they would have been invisible to those within the house, they were clearly important and suggest that cattle may have held a significance that far outweighed their mere value as a source of food.

The finds from Links of Noltland support the interpretation from Skara Brae and other sites that the Neolithic inhabitants of Orkney enjoyed a rich material life. There is much jewellery of highly polished bone, and also finely decorated pottery. Within Structure 8 a small, finely carved figurine of stone was uncovered and three others, two of stone and one of clay, have since been excavated, each from a separate structure. These figurines are simple and yet sophisticated in design. The first, known as the Orkney Venus, has clear representation of arms, clothing, facial features and even hair. It is the first time that we have a direct image of the prehistoric people of Scotland.

The remains at Links of Noltland are not formally laid out and visibility depends on current excavation and the state of the dunes. Information about the site is to be seen in the Westray Heritage Centre in Pierowall village.

5 The Stones of Stenness, Mainland   HY 306125

Historic Scotland; signposted; small car park.

The Stones of Stenness is a ceremonial site, in use by about 3100 BC. The first thing to be built here was the henge, comprising a circular earthen bank and ditch enclosing a central platform. Excavation has revealed this to have been an impressive monument: it was about 44 metres across and the ditch was cut into bedrock and over 2 metres deep and 7 metres wide. Hardly any trace of this original henge survives today. The bank encircled the outside of the henge, with one entrance causeway, and inside twelve standing stones were erected. At the centre of the circle there was a hearth-like stone setting, and various slots and pits for stone and timber structures were uncovered by excavation in the 1970s.

It is impossible now to reconstruct exactly what the different features at the centre of the monument looked like, and they are unlikely to have all been in use at the same time. The evidence suggests that a variety of ceremonial activities took place here.

Among the archaeological finds were sherds of pottery very similar to those used by the inhabitants of Skara Brae and Barnhouse. The impressive standing stones were erected at some stage during the life of the monument and are some of the tallest in Orkney. They may well have been erected over a considerable period of time rather than as a single design element.

Since Neolithic times the stone circle at Stenness has suffered much so that only a few stones survive today. Early in the last century the local tenant began to demolish the stones. His work was stopped, but at the turn of this century some stones were re-erected, perhaps with more artistic licence than archaeological knowledge and, in 1972, a horizontal 'altar' slab, which had been put into place as part of the 'reconstruction' work in 1906, was destroyed. Early records show the existence of outlying stones, but it is very difficult to be exactly sure of the original appearance of the monument. This gives a good idea of the problems affecting the study of all Orkney monuments, and it is important to remember that they have not necessarily always been as they appear today.

6 The Ring of Brodgar, Mainland   HY 294133

Historic Scotland; signposted; car park.

Brodgar is another impressive ceremonial monument, only a few 100 metres from the Stones of Stenness. It was probably in use in the mid-third millennium BC. It too comprises a circular earthen henge with a central platform about 105 metres in diameter surrounded by a ditch that would have been over 3 metres deep and 10 metres wide. Just inside the ditch a circle of sixty stones was erected, of which twenty-seven are still standing (several have been re-erected, and some are represented only by broken stumps).

The centre of the platform at Brodgar has never been excavated, so nothing is known about any stone and timber features that may have stood there, nor is there any detail of the activities that were carried out. Round the monument, however, lie the remains of over a dozen earthen burial mounds as well as various outlying stones. None of these have been excavated in modern times, and it is unlikely that they were all erected at the same time, but they do show the very great ritual value of the neck of land that stretched

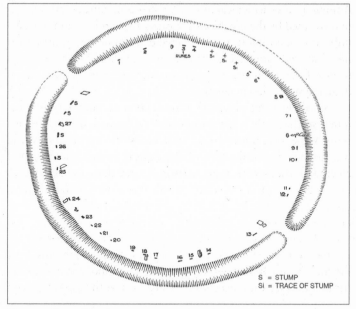

Figure 9. Ring of Brodgar.

between the lochs of Stenness and Harray. These monuments extend to the north of Brodgar as far as the henge of Bookan (of which very little remains to be seen today), and to the south as far as the Stones of Stenness and their outlying stone, the Barnhouse Stone. This area clearly comprised a great ceremonial centre for the Neolithic peoples of Orkney.

In the twelfth century, a Norse visitor to Brodgar left an early piece of graffiti when he carved his name, Bjorn, in code in runes on one of the stones.

7 Ness of Brodgar, Mainland   HY 303129

Site may be visited when open for excavation. Daily tours, viewing platform, car park. At all other times the site is covered and there is nothing to see.

The site at Ness of Brodgar has changed our understanding of Neolithic Britain, providing as it does evidence for monumental structures of a type and on a scale previously unimagined. Here, at the narrowest part of the isthmus between the lochs, excavation has revealed evidence for a walled enclosure surrounding a series of massive buildings, including two long structures subdivided into bays, several oval structures similar to the double 'house' at Barnhouse, and a great stone 'hall', comprising concentric walls that alternated with passageways to enclose a cruciform central space.

There is clear evidence that the structures at Ness of Brodgar were frequently rebuilt and remodelled and it is unlikely that all were in use at the same time. Nevertheless, the finds suggest that this was a high-status site and it may well have functioned as the heart of the ceremonial area that was previously defined by the stone circles. Evidence for the ritual slaughter of several hundred cattle adds to the picture of a very special place. Final analysis of Ness of Brodgar has still to be undertaken, so the precise interpretation of the life of the site and of the activities that took place here is still uncertain. The overall impression is of a ceremonial site, but it may be that some structures served a more domestic function, perhaps housing visitors to the area or workers. It should also be remembered that geophysical survey indicates a complexity of remains here, including other structures outside the wall.

It is a salutary lesson today that the interest previously ascribed to the stone circles may simply have been a reflection of their visibility into the twenty-first century rather than of their actual significance in the Neolithic.

8 The Ring of Bookan, Mainland   HY 283144

Private.

Almost nothing is now visible of this circular earthwork, which is generally interpreted as a henge monument relating to the ceremonial complex of Brodgar and Stenness.

9 The Watch Stone, Mainland   HY 306127

Private; use car park at the Stones of Stenness.

This impressive standing stone, part of the Brodgar and Stenness complex, lies right by the side of the road. It is over 6 metres tall.

Records suggest that there was a second stone here, destroyed during road building.

10 The Stane O'Quoybune, Mainland   HY 253263

Private; at side of road.

This is a single standing stone, though other standing stones and many burial mounds are recorded around Boardhouse Loch, where it stands. It has never been excavated, but this type of monument was apparently common in the second and third millennia BC.

11 The Stone of Setter, Eday   HY 564371

Private; at side of road.

This single stone stands 4.5 metres high, at the centre of a landscape containing several chambered tombs. It is clearly visible from quite a distance, and today weathering of the soft sandstone has given it a very distinctive appearance. Apart from the complex of Stenness and Brodgar, this is the tallest standing stone in Orkney.

12 The Mor Stane, Shapinsay   HY 524168

Private; at side of road.

This is an isolated standing stone some 3 metres high. There are signs of other prehistoric activity in the landscape, however, and a group of burial mounds may be seen just to the east.

13 Maeshowe, Mainland   HY 318127

Historic Scotland; signposted; car park; timed visits only.

The evidence suggests that the great tomb of Maeshowe was emptied long ago, but it remains one of the best-preserved architectural monuments of prehistory. The tomb is surrounded by a ditch and a low bank, and seems to have been built around 2700 BC. Maeshowe today appears as a massive grassy mound, covering an earth and stone barrow over a stone-built chamber, but it is clear that this is a complex monument and it may not always have had its present appearance, even in prehistory.

Recent excavation of a thin strip between the bank and the tomb revealed a stone hole on the grassy platform inside the ditch, and it is possible that the circular platform at Maeshowe originally contained a stone circle. It has also been suggested that the four huge upright stones inside the chamber may have stood in the open as free-standing stones before the chamber was built around them. This would certainly have helped with the alignment of the entrance passage, which has been carefully directed towards the midwinter solstice so that the setting sun shines onto the rear wall of the chamber.

Today the visitor enters through the original low, narrow passage, which is about 7 metres long. It is built of huge stone slabs and leads to the central chamber, which is 3.8 metres high. The walls are expertly laid of dry stone, and converge to form a square corbelled vault. In recent times Maeshowe was broken into through the roof, and the white-painted capping to the entrance hole may be seen at the centre of the vault. There are three side cells that open from the chamber, each with a chunky blocking stone on the floor outside. Unfortunately, there is no record of the original contents of the tomb, but it seems to have been designed to be opened and re-entered again and again. Just inside the entrance a triangular stone lies in a niche in the passage wall; this was the blocking stone and it would have been drawn forward in order to block access to the tomb.

The original occupants of Maeshowe may have long disappeared without any trace, but the tomb does contain a more personal touch from Neolithic times. Inscribed on the south-west upright slab within the chamber is a series of triangles and diamond shapes, along with various lines. These are characteristic of other examples of Neolithic art and, though nothing is known of their meaning or of the artist, they offer a direct link back some 4,000 years to a moment of inspiration, or other great motivation, when they were carefully carved with the point of a sharp stone tool.

Maeshowe is a large and complex site and it has been suggested that it would have taken over 100,000 man-hours to build. On this basis archaeologists have interpreted it as an important tomb, perhaps housing the remains of various generations of a high-ranking family and marking a community of status. Norse graffiti

Figure 10. Inside Maeshowe in the nineteenth century.

on the walls inside the chamber mention the removal of a great treasure from the tomb, but this is a puzzle because the original Neolithic builders of these monuments did not use metal. Some have suggested that the runic messages are not to be taken seriously, but others have pointed out that there is also evidence that the bank surrounding Maeshowe was rebuilt in the ninth century AD, and from this they suggest that the tomb might have been reused long after it was originally built, for the burial of an early Norse chieftain together with some precious grave goods.

14 Unstan, Mainland
HY 282117

Historic Scotland; signposted; small car park at the farm.

It is likely that the chambered tomb at Unstan was in use in the third millennium BC, but it is a different type of tomb from that at Maeshowe: a short entrance passage leads into a long dry-stone chamber set at right angles to the passage and divided into stalls by upright slabs of sandstone. In addition there is a small side cell

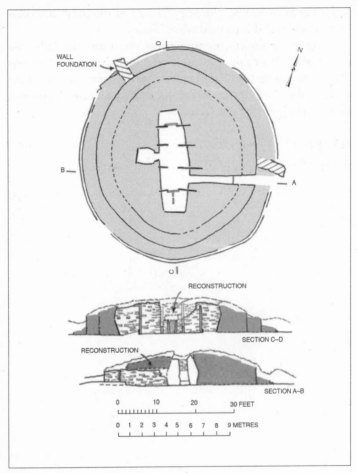

Figure 11. Unstan.

leading off the main chamber. Outside, the chamber is covered by a circular grass-covered cairn.

The tomb was excavated in 1884 and found to contain various burials in the compartments as well as the side cell. There were also the remains of many grave goods, in the form of pottery bowls (which have given their name to a specific design of round-bottomed Neolithic bowl: Unstan Ware), and some stone tools including arrowheads. The original roof of the tomb has been reconstructed, and is painted white inside.

Like many ancient monuments, Unstan was visited by the Norse, who left a runic inscription on one of the stones. This was discovered during consolidation work at the tomb, and it is now positioned as the lintel slab to the side chamber. There is also some more recent graffiti on this slab.

15 Cuween Hill Cairn, Mainland   HY 364127

Historic Scotland; signposted; car park; take a torch.

Cuween Hill Cairn was probably in use in the third millennium BC and is a Maeshowe-type tomb. It is entered (with difficulty)

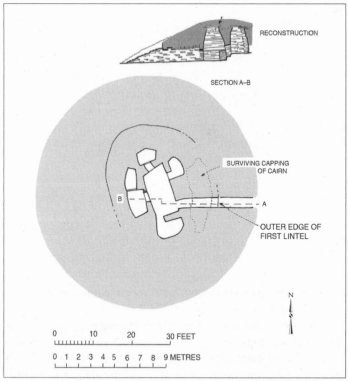

Figure 12. Cuween.

through a long low passage to reach a rectangular main chamber from which four side cells open. Cuween was built by skilled masons: they cut into bedrock in order to provide level foundations for the chamber and side cells, and then used local flagstones in order to construct the high roof on which the earthen mound is supported. The tomb was excavated at the turn of the last century (though it had already been explored) and it was found to contain the remains of at least eight human skeletons, together with some grave goods and many animal bones including twenty-four dog skulls (perhaps a totemic deposit).

16 Wideford Hill Cairn, Mainland   HY 409121

Historic Scotland; signposted; footpath to reach tomb, very steep return gradient.

Wideford Hill Cairn is a Maeshowe-type tomb, in use in the third millennium BC. The grass covering today does not cover all of the stonework, so that the original construction of the tomb is visible. The entrance passage is very low and narrow, so that a modern trap door and ladder have been inserted into the roof to provide access to the main chamber from which there are three side cells. Wideford Hill Cairn has been excavated more than once, but no burial remains were found, though it did seem as if the main chamber had been deliberately filled, from above, with rubble.

17 Quanterness, Mainland   HY 417129

In private garden.

Quanterness is another Maeshowe-type tomb and it was excavated in the 1970s to reveal much detail of the central chamber, which had six cells. Unlike most Orkney chambered tombs, Quanterness had suffered little past disturbance and so the burial deposits in the chambers were particularly well preserved, including many skeletons; these offered an interesting example of how the tomb was used.

Only part of the material inside the tomb at Quanterness was excavated, in order to leave something for posterity when better archaeological techniques might be available, but in the sample

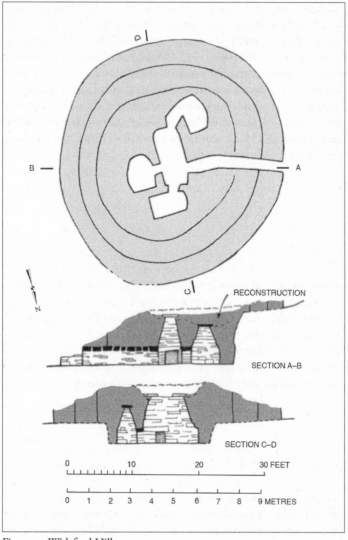

Figure 13. Wideford Hill.

examined the remains of at least 157 people were found. These bodies included men, women and children, and it has been estimated that the tomb may have held the remains of about 400 people in total. Although this may seem like a sizeable population, it must be remembered that the burials took place over a long period of time and may have represented only certain members of the community. Mixed in with the human remains were bones from various birds and animals (there were remains from both domestic species, such as sheep, pigs and cattle, and wild species, such as otter, fox and deer). The artefacts from the tomb comprise a variety of Neolithic goods, including decorated sherds of pottery, worked flint and chert, and bone pins and beads.

The excavation also revealed that Quanterness had traces of later activity from the Iron Age, when a roundhouse had been built on the eastern side of the tomb. In order to do this the Iron Age builders had had to demolish part of the outer mound of the cairn over the tomb.

18 Head of Work, Mainland   HY 484138

Private.

This is a long cairn, with projecting horns at either end. It is now grass covered and so it is quite hard to make out the original shape of the cairn. At the wider end there is an oval cairn, from which various stone slabs protrude. These probably mark the position of the chamber, but the cairn has been dug into at different times and disturbed so that nothing is known of its original contents or form. The tomb lies at the highest point of a low peninsula and there are good views out to sea to the island of Shapinsay across the sound.

19 Isbister, South Ronaldsay   ND 470845

Private; signposted; car park; visitor centre.

Isbister is an interesting tomb. It is a Stalled Cairn, in use from the late fourth millennium BC into the third millennium, but there are also influences from the Maeshowe tradition of cairn building. The main chamber is divided by pairs of upright flagstones, and there are also three side cells. At either end there is a shelved compartment. The original roof was removed from the cairn in antiquity and it seems to have been deliberately filled with rubble, probably when it went out of use about 2500 BC.

Figure 14.
A plan of the
tomb at
Quanterness,
published by
the Rev. Barry
in 1805.

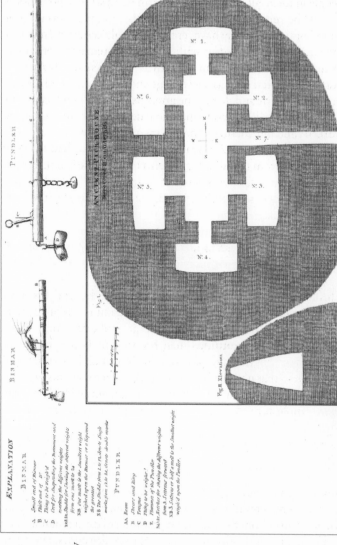

Isbister was excavated in recent times, most recently in 1982, and, as the deposits were well preserved and generally in good condition, a wealth of detail about the use of the tomb has been revealed. The remains of many skeletons were found here. There were bones from about 340 people, both adults and children, though they were no longer preserved as complete skeletons, and some parts of the tomb held specific bones such as the deposits of skulls which lay in two of the side cells. Analysis indicates that many of the individuals buried in the tomb were suffering from trauma or diseases such as scurvy. There were also many grave goods of both pottery and stone. In addition, there were numerous animal bones, including various deposits of bones from white-tailed eagles. It has been suggested that these were a totemic deposit relating to the identity of the community that used the tomb. This has led to the popular name for Isbister: the Tomb of the Eagles. In view of this suggestion, the spectacular location of the tomb, at the edge of steep sea cliffs such as those frequented by the white-tailed eagle, is particularly interesting.

The museum on site houses a display of artefacts from the tomb, together with information about life in the Neolithic.

20 Banks, South Ronaldsay   ND 458834

Private; signposted; car park and bistro.

The tomb at Banks was discovered in 2010 and excavation began shortly after. Excitingly, the tomb has survived with little disturbance since it was closed during the Neolithic and waterlogged conditions mean that preservation is very good. Excavation is still ongoing, but already the remains of many individuals have been recovered, as well as much environmental material and artefacts including decorated pottery.

The tomb at Banks is of the Maeshowe type, with six side cells. There is a small display of finds, and guided tours are available.

21 The Dwarfie Stane, Hoy   HY 243004

Historic Scotland; signposted; footpath from road.

The Dwarfie Stane is quite unlike any other Orcadian Neolithic tomb, indeed it is unlike anything in Scotland, but parallels away from Orkney suggest that it was carved sometime in the third millennium BC. It comprises a huge block of red sandstone, which has been hollowed out in the centre to form a small chamber with a cell on either side. It has been carefully made and the marks from the stone tools used by its makers may be seen on the roof of the southernmost cell.

There is no record of the excavation of this tomb, though the roof was broken through at some stage (it is now restored), and no

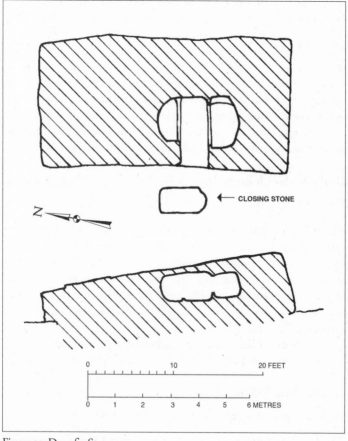

Figure 15. Dwarfie Stane.

record of burials or of grave goods. There is a large blocking stone by the entrance, which was apparently in place in the doorway in the sixteenth century.

Those who made the Dwarfie Stane took a lot of time and trouble, and it is odd to find something quite so different from Orkney's general Neolithic tombs here on Hoy. Indeed, few chambered tombs have so far been discovered on Hoy. Some comparisons may be drawn between the Dwarfie Stane and the more standard burial rites of Neolithic Orkney, in the use of side cells and a main blocking stone, but there is a complete lack of information as to how it was used and why there are no others. Were the Neolithic inhabitants of Hoy responding to their more mountainous environment? Or had they been in touch with ideas from overseas? We can never know. They have left us with a spectacular Neolithic mystery.

The Dwarfie Stane is an impressive monument and, not surprisingly, it has attracted much graffiti. On the uphill end is a double inscription, carved in Persian and reversed Latin, made by one William Mounsey, a solicitor from Cumbria. He was a colourful eccentric who had spent much time as a soldier in the Middle East where he worked as a British spy in Persia and where he came into contact with many Jews. In the East, Mounsey made a study of Jewish history, culture, and religion, and on his return to Britain he took to wearing Jewish clothes and left many enigmatic inscriptions (in a variety of languages) and rock carvings along the length of his home river, the Eden. Mounsey's Latinised signature was frequently incorporated, backwards, into these inscriptions, and, though he left no records of his trip to Orkney, the similarity between the message on the Dwarfie Stane (dated to 1850), and his Cumbrian relics is striking. On the stone he records how he spent two nights there and learned patience; this is often taken to be a reference to the tenacity of the local midges.

22 Taversoe Tuick, Rousay   HY 425276

Historic Scotland; signposted.

Taversoe Tuick is an unusual tomb in that it has two storeys with separate entrances. It dates to the third millennium BC. The lower tomb was originally entered by a long passage from the downhill side, leading into a chamber which is divided into four shelved compartments. The upper tomb was quite separate from the lower, and different in design: it was entered from uphill, along a shorter passage, leading to a chamber composed of two rounded compartments. In prehistory there would have been no access between the two storeys, but today a hatch leads down from one tomb to the other. The upper chamber was subsequently altered by the addition of three stone cists, but these have since been removed.

The tomb was discovered at the end of the last century when Lady Burroughs, the wife of the local landowner, decided to use its prominent knowe as the site for a garden seat, and since then it has been excavated in more detail. The lower chamber contained the remains of several skeletons and in the upper chamber the cists contained cremated bone from a child and at least two adults. There were also many grave goods.

At the edge of the tomb, close to the downhill end of the lower passage, a miniature chamber had been built and was found to contain three Neolithic pots, but no burials. This chamber is thought to have been used during the rituals that took place in the main tomb.

23 Blackhammer, Rousay   HY 414276

Historic Scotland; signposted; footpath from road.

Blackhammer is a Stalled Cairn, dating to the third millennium BC, with a central chamber 13 metres long, divided by upright flagstones into seven compartments. It is now entered through a hatch in the modern concrete capping.

The stonework at Blackhammer was very carefully laid in groups of sloping slabs on the outside of the cairn in order to form a triangular decorative pattern round the edges of the tomb. Inside, excavators in the 1930s found the remains of two skeletons, together with some grave goods and animal bone. The original entrance passage led in from one of the long sides of the cairn and was deliberately blocked when the tomb went out of use. The blocking included stones set at an angle to match the decorative patterning round the face of the cairn.

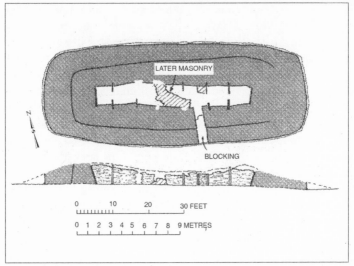

Figure 16. Blackhammer.

24 The Knowe of Yarso, Rousay　　　　　　　HY 404279

Historic Scotland; signposted; footpath from road.

This is a Stalled Cairn. It dates to the third millennium BC and, like Blackhammer, has decorative slanting stonework round the outside. The chamber is still entered at one end by the original passage and it is divided into four compartments by upright slabs. The Knowe of Yarso was excavated in the 1930s when the remains of twenty-nine skeletons were found, with many of the skulls set along the base of the walls in the innermost compartment. There were also some grave goods, including many stone tools, and many animal bones, mainly of red deer. At least thirty-six deer skeletons were represented and it has been suggested that the deer may have been the animal totem for the community who used the tomb.

25 Midhowe, Rousay　　　　　　　HY 372304

Historic Scotland; signposted; footpath from road.

Midhowe is a magnificent Stalled Cairn, dating to the third millen-

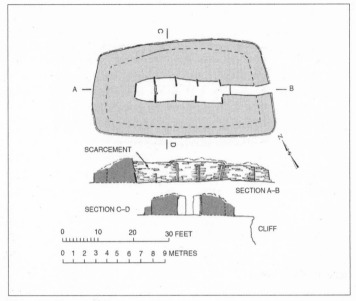

Figure 17. Knowe of Yarso.

nium BC and lying, unusually for Rousay, low down right on the coast. In common with some of the other Rousay tombs, the outer face of the cairn is decorated with angular set slabs to give a herring-bone effect. The original entrance passage led into the chamber at one end, but was deliberately blocked in prehistory, when the tomb went out of use. The chamber is 23 metres long and was divided into twelve compartments, many of which had stone shelves or benches. The excavations in the 1930s discovered the remains of twenty-five skeletons, including two children. Some of the bones were still lying on or below the stone benches where, it seems, that their bodies had been laid to rest. There were also various grave goods of stone and pottery, as well as animal bones. The chamber had been filled with rubble when the tomb went out of use.

Today, Midhowe is encased in a large stone and metal hangar, inside this there are metal catwalks which allow a particularly good view of the tomb. On a warm sunny day it seems to have a life of its own as it lies basking inside this strange modern housing.

26 Vinquoy, Eday

HY 560381

OIC; signposted; footpath to site.

Vinquoy is a Maeshowe-type tomb with four cells leading off a central chamber. It dates to the third millennium BC and is built on the slope, just below the crest of the hill. This gives marvellous views across the islands, but it meant that the builders had to dig out the side of the hill to provide a level floor so that the tomb is semi-subterranean. Vinquoy was excavated in the mid-nineteenth century, but there is no record of what was found. It must have stood at least 3 metres high, and is still well preserved. It has been restored, and today the chamber is protected by a clear plastic roof.

27 Calf of Eday Long Cairn; Calf of Eday

HY 578386

Private; boats over to the island may be arranged from Calfsound in Eday.

This is an interesting tomb because it shows how the design of some monuments could be dramatically altered throughout the long periods they were in use. It is quite ruinous and covered in vegetation today, but it is still possible to make out the remains of the chambers.

The tomb builders first built a small oval cairn in which lay a chamber, subdivided into two by upright slabs. Then a larger long cairn was built up against this, with another entrance passage leading in from the far end to a quite separate long chamber, which was divided into four stalls. The remains of stone benches and various internal fittings were discovered inside this chamber when it was excavated in the 1930s. Finally, a rectangular cairn was built over the whole monument.

Poor preservation conditions meant that there was little detail of the burials within either tomb when it was excavated, but associated artefacts included much pottery and worked flint as well as two stone axes which were found lying on one of the benches in the stalled chamber.

28 Calf of Eday, North-West HY 578385

Private; boats over to the island may be arranged from Calfsound in Eday; care needed.

This is a round cairn that may be entered, though it is not in state or island care. There is an irregular central chamber, divided into four compartments by upright slabs. It was 'examined' long ago and there is little information about its original contents, though it seems to have contained stone benches and a blocking stone at the entrance when it was first found.

29 Calf of Eday, South-East HY 579385

Private; boats over to the island may be arranged from Calfsound in Eday; care needed.

This round cairn lies close to the preceding site, and may also be entered with care. It is a semi-subterranean monument: the passage and chamber were sunk below ground, though the mound was raised above ground level. Like its neighbour, the central chamber is divided into four compartments by upright slabs. This site was also opened early, and there is little information regarding its original state or contents.

30 Quoyness, Sanday HY 676377

Historic Scotland; signposted; footpath to the site.

This is a Maeshowe-type tomb, dating to the early third millennium BC. It is a complex structure, and has been laid out today to give an idea of the complexity of its building, rather than of the original appearance of the tomb, which must have been impressive. A wide stone platform surrounds the central cairn stonework, and there is a long passage (now roofed for less than half its original length) leading to the chamber. The chamber stands to its original height of 4 metres, though it is no longer roofed across. Six side cells open from the central chamber, but there is very little information from the nineteenth-century excavations that took place here. It is clear that there were the remains of many human burials, some in four of the side cells and others in a circular stone-lined pit in the floor

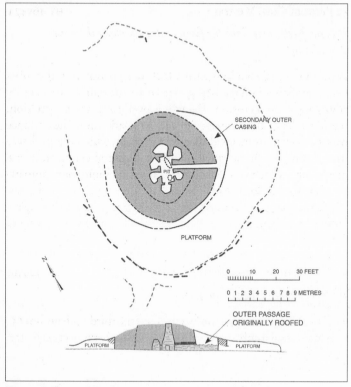

Figure 18. Quoyness.

of the chamber. The burials included both adults and children and were accompanied by animal bones as well as objects of stone and pottery.

31 Lamb Ness, Stronsay   HY 689212

Private; coastal walk to site.

Just back from the shore lie the grassed-over remains of an oval cairn in which the remains of five stone slabs can be seen. These slabs divided the chamber into at least three stalls. Another mound, also with protruding slabs, lies close by, but archaeologists interpret this as the remains of a domestic structure.

32 Point of Cott, Westray HY 465474

*Private; park away from the farm and walk along the coast;
care needed.*

Point of Cott is a Stalled Cairn which was excavated in the 1980s
because of the damage being caused to the cairn structure by
advancing coastal erosion. Today it is overgrown with vegetation,
but it is still possible to make out the main structure. The entrance
passage opened from a wide curved forecourt, which was probably
used during the burial rituals. It led to a central chamber, over 8
metres long, which was divided by upright slabs into four compartments with a curious double box set into the inner compartment.
Inside the chamber the excavators found bones from twelve people
(adults and children), as well as objects of stone and pottery and
animal bones.

33 The Holm of Papa Westray South HY 509518

Historic Scotland; boat from pier.

This is a Maeshowe-type tomb, dating to the third millennium BC.
It is an unusual tomb because the central chamber is over 20 metres

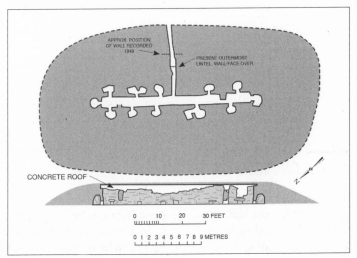

Figure 19. Holm of Papa Westray South.

long, and there are twelve side cells, two of which are double. Inside the tomb there are several decorated stone slabs to the south of the passage and in the southern end of the main chamber, where a lintel at the entrance to one of the cells has been decorated with pecked dots and arcs. These motifs are interpreted as 'eyebrow' motifs, similar to those seen on the figurine from Links of Noltland; they seem to be Neolithic in design, and similar patterns have been found in some of the Irish chambered tombs. The Holm of Papa Westray South was excavated in the mid-nineteenth century and nothing is known of its original contents. It is entered today through a hatchway in the roof.

34 The Holm of Papa Westray North   HY 504522

Private.

In contrast to its sister tomb on this small island, this was a Stalled Cairn with a central chamber about 5 metres long, entered at one end. The chamber is divided into four compartments, with a small end cell opposite the entrance passage, and the mound above was rectangular. Holm of Papa Westray North has recently been exca-

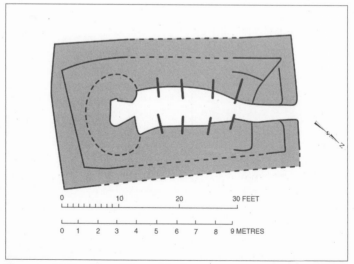

Figure 20. Holm of Papa Westray North.

vated and was found to contain the remains of over eight burials (both adults and children), as well as various animal bones and grave goods. There was evidence that the tomb had been infilled with earth and stones after it went out of use, and to do this the roof had been taken off. It was in use in the third millennium BC.

The First Metalworkers:
Bronze Age Orkney

Bronze Age Changes

The lifestyle of the Neolithic farmers was highly successful. Permanent villages of sophisticated architecture sprang up, and there was the leisure, organisation and willingness to work together to build a variety of larger monuments. The evidence suggests that Orkney pioneered some of the developments that were to take hold further south in mainland Britain. But change is inevitable, and to the south in mainland Scotland it was not long in coming. Towards the end of the third millennium BC new goods and materials were being imported into the country. The most radical change in material culture was the introduction of metal, usually in the form of copper and bronze daggers and axes, but this was also accompanied by new forms of pottery (deeper, elaborately decorated, finely-made vessels known as 'beakers'), and there is clear evidence for wide-reaching change throughout society.

The origin of this change is still a point of academic debate, but there is some evidence to link the new way of life and goods with incomers (so-called 'Beaker Folk') from the Low Countries, across the North Sea. Wherever they came from and however they spread, it seems that these changes were slow to reach Orkney, perhaps because of the distances that had to be travelled. Nevertheless sherds of the new-style 'beaker' pottery do turn up on many sites by the end of the third millennium BC and there is increasing evidence for activity on beaker-related sites. Metal goods were scarce at first in Orkney, and few are found in association with other archaeological remains so it is difficult to interpret how they were used. Doubtless, they were initially seen as rare and prestigious items.

Some archaeologists have suggested that Orcadians at this time were essentially conservative and reluctant to accept the new ideas.

This is perhaps not surprising, given the richness of the Neolithic lifestyle that had been established, but the information from increasing excavation on Bronze Age sites now refutes this. Changes in settlement pattern, house types and material goods away from the monumental remains of Skara Brae and the great tombs may well mean that there is less detail about the lifestyle of the Bronze Age Orcadians, but this does not mean that their life was any the less rich or sophisticated, and recent excavations are now starting to fill out the picture.

Orkney has its own seams of copper, but there is no evidence that these were exploited in prehistory, and it has been argued that most metal goods were probably imported into the islands. The evidence for local metalworking that does exist comes from later in prehistory (one stone axe mould is the only hint of early working that exists). If metal goods had to be imported, this might account for the rarity of Bronze Age metalwork in Orkney.

It was not only the introduction of metal goods that affected material life, however, as different pottery types became common, and there were new types of flaked stone tools. The intricate villages of Skara Brae and elsewhere seem to have gone out of use, and the existing evidence for Bronze Age settlement in Orkney suggests that people lived in individual farmsteads scattered across the islands and comprising stone-built dwellings, often with an associated outbuilding.

If Orkney in the Bronze Age was conservative in one way, it was not so in others. There is evidence that the great tomb at Pierowall Quarry was deliberately destroyed at this time, and similar changes were taking place to other chambered tombs. At Quoyness and many other tombs the chamber was permanently sealed and in some cases backfilled. Individual burials were often inserted at this time, perhaps as a closing act. Some tombs did remain in use, but it seems that the focus of this use shifted so that collective burial was no longer regarded as important. Instead, individuals were buried on their own. Sherds of beaker pottery found in the closing layers of many tombs suggest that this sort of pottery had ceremonial as well as domestic importance.

At the same time different changes were also taking place to other ceremonial sites: the site at Ness of Brodgar seems to have been slighted and abandoned; at the Stones of Stenness the ditch was dug and standing stones erected; at Maeshowe a wide, deep ditch was dug round the tomb. It is hard to interpret what was going on, but there were clearly major alterations to ceremonial life, and it is likely that these reflected alterations in other aspects of society. It has been suggested that the shift in emphasis away from collective to single burial reflects the rise of a more hierarchical society with individual leaders.

The Bronze Age was not only a time of change in society. It was also a period of great climatic change. It has long been noted that peat growth started about now in many parts of Scotland, and this indicates a considerable increase in rainfall. Other palaeo environmental work has recorded increased storminess on the west coast of Scotland, as well as gradually declining temperatures. In 1159 BC the volcano Hekla in Iceland erupted, and this is likely to have had an adverse effect on climate as dust circled the atmosphere and blocked out sunlight. The cumulative effect of these changes is such that some modern researchers have referred to possibly catastrophic results.

In the face of this climatic deterioration it would have been hard for life on the Bronze Age farms to continue as before. Population had been increasing, and in Orkney, as elsewhere in Britain, there is evidence that much upland land was taken into cultivation, only to be abandoned as conditions worsened later on in the period. Pressure on, and therefore competition for, land doubtless increased, and people had to adapt their ways in order to survive.

Domestic Life

The record of Bronze Age settlement in Orkney has only recently been fully recognised, and to date few dwelling sites have been excavated. The village sites that were the norm in the Neolithic, such as Skara Brae and Barnhouse, were abandoned and families moved into individual farmsteads scattered across the islands. Elsewhere in Britain small communities of timber roundhouses were the norm, and in Orkney similar houses of stone, or stone and turf were built. At Links of Noltland in Westray at least ten of these dwellings have been excavated, sometimes in pairs with a smaller building apparently serving as a workshop or byre. At Tofts Ness in Sanday the animals were accommodated in a small annex to the main house. Both sites comprise agricultural landscapes with clear evidence of farming both animals and crops.

In this period a new type of site known as a 'burnt mound' appears and the evidence suggests that these were related to everyday life. Burnt mounds, as their name implies, comprise mounds of blackened, charcoal-enriched soil mixed with heat-cracked, fist-sized stones and ash. They vary in size and shape, and are not confined to Orkney; others occur across Scotland and also in Ireland. Excavation has revealed the remains of activity areas within, or sometimes to one side of, the mound. The working area is often paved, with a hearth and a large pit, which is usually stone-lined in Orkney. Other stone features are common, and the area is usually surrounded by a low stone wall, which has led some archaeologists to suggest that the whole structure was roofed like a house, although others dispute this. Burnt mounds are always situated close to fresh water.

There are many interpretations for the burnt mounds and, of course, they may well have served different functions on different occasions. Some are interpreted as cooking places where stones could be heated and placed in the pit, which would contain food, probably meat, together with water. This is a very traditional method of cooking, recorded in early Irish history as a communal feast, and used into the eighteenth century in the Hebrides. Cooking in this way still takes place elsewhere, for example in Polynesia and in Chile where the recipe for curanto, a popular southern dish, involves digging a hole 1 metre in diameter and at least 25 centimetres deep. 'A fire is lit in the pit, and stones are placed on top to heat up. Once the stones are red hot, the ashes are swept out and the pit is lined with leaves; now a large quantity of mixed shellfish (45 kilos) and meat (5 kilos) may be placed on top. This is well sealed with leaves and earth so that no steam can escape, and in just over an hour it is opened to reveal a delicious stew'*. Interestingly, no water is added. This is a common dish at markets and

*From: Huneeus, P., *Manual Basico de Cocina* (Editora Neueva Generacion Ltda, Santiago 1993).

fairs, and one that the author has frequently enjoyed! (These quantities would make a curanto for about twenty people.)

Some burnt mounds may have been associated with prehistoric brewing; others have been interpreted as bath structures or saunas. It is hard to be specific about their function because the main evidence lies in the combination of water and heat. The use of stones to heat water and the impact of repeated heating and cooling resulted in the accumulation of shattered heating stones, and in this way a mound of old, discarded material and hearth sweepings would gradually accumulate over the years.

There are many interpretations for the burnt mounds and, of course, they may well have served different functions on different occasions. Burnt mounds are a common feature of the Bronze Age landscape across the islands and, while they may give us an insight into one aspect of life in the Bronze Age, they do not seem to have been actual dwelling places. Presumably people did not live too far away, and they may well have served a communal, central, function.

Bronze Age Ceremony and Burial

In addition to the emerging evidence of settlement and the enigmatic burnt mounds, there is archaeological information that relates to other aspects of life in the Bronze Age. The great ceremonial centres were still in use, though, as noted above, the rituals involved had clearly changed. There is also plenty of evidence relating to burial.

The burial monuments of the Bronze Age were smaller affairs than their predecessors, though they involved a greater effort per burial. Most Bronze Age burials still comprised mounds of earth ('barrows') or of stones ('cairns'), raised over stone-lined boxes ('cists'). Each mound usually contained a central cist and there were sometimes others inserted into or beside the mound at a later date. Each cist usually (but not always) contained one body. In addition, cists have been found that are not covered by a mound. Both burial mounds and cists usually occur in groups (cemeteries).

Within the cist, the body was generally laid to rest with grave goods, such as a flint knife and a pot which may have held liquor or food. Some people were laid to rest simply, with the body crouched up to fit into the tomb, but others were given a new rite: their bodies were cremated after death so that the fragments of burnt bone could be gathered to be placed in the cist. Although there are multiple burials, the focus in the Bronze Age seems to have lain much more upon the individual, or the individual family. There are none of the great charnel houses of the Neolithic.

Many groups of barrows and cairns occur across Orkney, and there are also isolated monuments. One of the most prominent and largest groups occurs round the Ring of Brodgar, with some to the north as far as the Ring of Bookan, and to the south round Maeshowe. The strip of land between the lochs of Stenness and Harray obviously continued in importance long after the Neolithic.

Another group of burial mounds lay at Lingafold on the shores of the Loch of Stenness. Excavation here revealed an interesting variety of mounds and cists, with evidence for various different types of burial activity, including cremation. One cist contained a huge steatite urn, the material for which must have come from the Shetland Isles to the north. There was no evidence for Bronze Age dwellings, but a stone-slabbed path led into the cemetery from the west.

A concentration of Bronze Age burial mounds has also long been known in the sand dunes of Sandfiold at the Bay of Skaill, to the north-west of Skara Brae. Many of these were examined as early as 200 years ago, and little is known of their contents, but more recently quarrying work has revealed a different sort of tomb here. The tomb comprised a stone cist, slightly larger than normal, set into a chamber cut into the rock. On one side of the cist the side slab could be lowered, and thus the tomb could be opened again and again. Inside there were three burials: a pottery vessel containing the cremated bones of an adult between 25 and 40 years old; the unburnt bones of a woman together with an 8-month foetus; and a heap of cremated fragments from the burial of a man of between 25 and 30 years. Radiocarbon dating suggested that the tomb had been in use *c.* 2000 BC.

The Sandfiold cist is, at present, unique, but it was completely hidden below the present ground surface, and others may well await discovery. There is at least one other unusual tomb from Orkney at this time. This is the site of Knowes of Trotty, which comprises a group of burial mounds just below the high ground to the northern end of the Loch of Harray. The mounds here are particularly large, but apart from that they appear unremarkable. They were opened and explored long ago and there is no record of their contents. However, at one end lies the greatest mound, examined in 1858 by a local archaeologist, George Petrie. Inside, he discovered the usual stone cist with cremated remains, but in one corner of this lay a stone slab on which there were four decorated gold discs and twenty-one pieces of amber.

No other burials have been recorded from Orkney with such rich grave goods as those from the Knowes of Trotty and they point to some of the long-distance links of life in the Bronze Age. The gold has been analysed, and came from a Scottish source, perhaps that also used for the gold decoration on the hilt of a bronze dagger from Fife. The style and manufacture of the discs, however, indicate close links further afield, with the Wessex area in the south of England, where similar goods were produced at this time. The amber also suggests links with necklaces from the south of Britain, though the material itself may have come from as far away as Scandinavia.

Recent excavation and analysis suggests that the Knowes of Trotty was the burial site of a prestigious individual, and other rich burials may well have been discovered in the past. There is little detail about the occupants of the Sandfiold cist, and no information on those whose burials crowd the land around Maeshowe and Brodgar. But these tombs, and the objects within them, are all indications that society in the Bronze Age was neither simple nor insular.

BRONZE AGE SITES (see map, p. xxix)

Although the pattern of settlement seems to have changed in the Bronze Age, the great ceremonial circles and standing stones continued in use, albeit with some modification to both their structure and presumably to the ceremonies practised within them. The visitor to both the Ring of Brodgar and the Stones of Stenness can, therefore, get an idea of the Bronze Age landscape of Orkney, especially if the surrounding earthen barrow groups are taken into consideration.

1 Liddle Burnt Mound, South Ronaldsay ND 464841

Private; signposted; car park; visitor centre.

The mound of burnt stones that covered this site was originally about 2 metres high. It has now been cleared by excavation to reveal the structure that lay beneath. This structure was built of stone and comprises an oval wall, now standing to about 1 metre, with various alcoves and recesses. At the centre lies a large stone-lined trough, and to one side a hearth lies in an alcove in the wall.

Today Liddle lies within a poorly-drained, boggy depression; water was clearly central to its function, and the tank at the centre could be drained through a gully which ran to the outside of the building. When discovered, the trough was still half-full with burnt stones, and the mound around the outside of the walls also comprised burnt stones and ash. This site is interpreted by the excavator as a cooking place, used again and again over the years, perhaps for communal feasts, or more simply as a central place for the local Bronze Age farmers.

Some burnt mound structures seem to have been unroofed (see Meur, below), but it is likely that Liddle was roofed in turf or thatch over a timber framework. No trace of associated dwellings has been discovered, but they may well lie close-by. Liddle was in use in the early first millennium BC.

2 Knowes of Trotty, Mainland HY 342172

Private, access allowed by footpath from car park
at HY 334164.

There are twelve barrows here, dating to the early second millennium BC. The largest lies at the north end of the group and, when excavated in the nineteenth century, was found to contain a substantial cist burial with cremated remains, four gold discs and amber beads and pendants. Such a rich burial is very unusual at this date and indicates that the primary burial must have been that of someone of very high social status.

Recent archaeological work shows that the cemetery was once more extensive and included a charnel or ceremonial house, and up to 20 barrows. In addition there were various settings and sitings for funeral pyres. This was clearly an important centre in the Bronze Age.

The grave goods from the Knowes of Trotty are interesting in another sense because they indicate links with southern England. The amber for the jewellery is likely to have come from the Baltic, but the style of the necklace suggests that it was made in the south. In Scotland, this sort of necklace was usually made in jet. This argument is supported by the gold discs, which are thought to have been button covers; they are made in a technique also used on English material of a comparable date, though analysis of the metal indicates that it was Scottish gold. It has been suggested that these objects show the influence of training in craftwork from the Wessex area (where other burials with similar rich goods were taking place at the time) and they may well have been made there and imported to the north. It is a clear indication that the individual buried at Knowes of Trotty was not only wealthy, but also part of a wide-ranging network. Through this they had access to rare and expensive materials and goods.

3 Kirbuster Hill, Mainland   HY 284263

Private.

There are at least ten barrows of varying size in this cemetery. It lies just below the summit of Kirbuster Hill, between the lochs of Boardhouse and Hundland, and in an area known for other Bronze Age monuments: barrows; standing stones; and burnt mounds. In the Bronze Age, areas such as this were clearly not as marginal as they seem today.

4 Ravie Hill, Mainland   HY 267251

Private.

This is another barrow cemetery in the Boardhouse area. At least nine barrows lie between the road and the loch. Most were 'examined' long ago and nothing is known of their contents, but one has been excavated more recently. The burial comprised a stone cist inside a circular kerb of small stones and it contained the cremated remains of two adults, a man and a woman, as well as the remains of a red deer and some artefacts including pottery and a stone disc.

5 Meur Burnt Mound, Sanday HY 747 457

On the shore at the side of the road.

The burnt mound at Meur is likely to date top around 1000 BC. It was excavated in 2005 in advance of the destruction of the site by winter storms. Only fragments of the site now remain, vulnerable to further erosion. Like other burnt mounds a large stone trough lay at the centre of the site, but the overall structure was defined by walling of upright slabs so it is unlikely that it was ever roofed. Various compartments surrounded the trough, and there was a cistern with a drainage system. Much of the filling had already been eroded by the time the excavation took place, but bones from cattle, sheep and fish were recovered, together with worked stone and sherds of pottery.

Some of the superstructure of the site is to be moved and reconstructed as part of a burnt mound exhibition in the grounds of the Sanday Heritage Centre at Lady in order to facilitate preservation. Elements such as the cistern and burnt material will remain visible in the eroding coastal section.

6 Elsness Barrows, Sanday HY 673376

Private.

On the peninsula of Elsness to the south of the chambered tomb of Quoyness lie a group of mounds that would seem to date to the second millennium BC. While some of these have traces of internal cists that suggest they relate to burial (and the nearby large Neolithic tomb of Quoyness should be noted), the whole area is indicative of an extensive farming landscape with traces of Bronze Age settlement.

7 Tofts Ness, Sanday HY 760470

Private.

An extensive group of cairns and mounds lies on the peninsula of Tofts Ness at the north-east end of Sanday. They are associated with agricultural remains such as banks and enclosures. The whole area gives a good example of a prehistoric landscape and this is something that has only survived in a few parts of Britain. Recent excavation and survey work here has shown that the remains relate to settlement as well as farming and that this activity dates back to the Neolithic, continuing through the Bronze Age and into the Iron Age. Among the domestic structures excavated were the stone foundations of a large roundhouse. It was divided radially into several rooms and had a central hearth as well as drains. Next to it was a small oval structure incorporating a large stone-lined tank and this has been interpreted by some as the site of a burnt mound-type cooking place, though there was no associated mound of cooking stones.

8 Warness, Eday

HY 553284

Private.

This low mound is the site of a burnt mound. It is possible to see the build-up of burnt stones in the bank of the stream which cuts it.

9 Holm of Faray

HY 527384

Private.

The remains of two structures, identified as Bronze Age houses, may be seen at the south-west corner of this tiny island. They have not been excavated, but it is possible to make out one clear oval building with internal partitions, and a narrow passage that leads to the other structure.

10 Monkshouses, Auskerry

HY 672163

Private.

This is a classic example of an unexcavated burnt mound site. Today the ground beside it is boggy, and the crescentic shape of the mound can still be made out.

11 Auskerry

Private.

The remains of two stone structures, identified as a Bronze Age farmstead, lie on the slopes of the hillside. They are connected by a narrow passage, and around them lie traces of ancient field dykes.

12 Knowe of Backiskaill, Papa Westray

Private.

A prominent mound nearly 3 metres high is the site of a burnt mound and gives a good idea of the appearance of these monuments before they have been excavated and laid out for public display, as at Liddle Farm. Of course, most are not as well preserved as this one. The mound is crescentic in shape and covered with vegetation, though some protruding stonework, presumably from internal structures, may be seen, as well as the general burnt debris from the cooking stones.

Fighting Farmers:
Iron Age Orkney

Whereas Iron Age Orkney was once known through its settlements and the implied hierarchies of its social structure, recent excavation has shown that there was greater depth to society here. There is increasing evidence for a range of settlement types. There was, perhaps, a ceremonial focus to rival that of Neolithic Orkney, at Mine Howe, and there were clearly local centres that acted as places of burial and remembrance.

Roundhouses

The scarcity of domestic remains discovered from Bronze Age Orkney is not replicated in the period that was to follow: the Iron Age. By the mid-first millennium BC people were building, and living in, substantial stone-built roundhouses with internal stone fittings. These have often come to light by accident during the excavation of some other site, and few have been deliberately excavated, but archaeologists have suggested that several settlements of dwellings like these may have existed in Orkney.

At Quanterness, just south of the main road between Finstown and Kirkwall, excavation of a chambered tomb in the early 1970s revealed a roundhouse built into the entrance area of the tomb about 700 BC, some 2,000 years after the tomb had gone out of use. By this time the tomb would have appeared as a stony, grass-covered mound and it provided a convenient supply of building stone for the local Iron Age inhabitants. They raised thick stone walls and also used the dismantled cairn stones for internal divisions and fittings.

In the islands to the north, another roundhouse built of tomb material has been excavated at Pierowall Quarry in Westray. Here the house lay on top of the tomb mound, which had been levelled and paved in order to provide a floor. This house dates to about

600 BC and seems to be of a similar age to another structure in Mainland, at the Bu, just outside Stromness. At the Bu the house comprised a very substantial stone wall, at least 5 metres thick, and it is interpreted as a defended structure. It was partially paved inside and was divided into various small rooms around the edge. Internally, there were many stone features including a large hearth with a tank to one side. Many domestic artefacts were recovered from the inside, particularly around the hearth area, and in some of the outer compartments. The house at the Bu comprises one of the earliest examples of a defended settlement in Orkney, and this, in itself, is an indication of changing times.

Not far from the Bu lay the site of Howe, where excavations revealed a complex sequence of activity, starting with a Neolithic burial complex. Later developments here, from the eighth century BC, included a group of small houses and then the construction of a substantial roundhouse within an enclosure defended by walls and ditches. This roundhouse was not unlike that at the Bu and it contained similar internal detail. Over it lay the solid structure of a broch.

Brochs

The Howe and Bu roundhouses were considerable structures, and houses like these seem to have developed into even more imposing round buildings: brochs. Brochs were built across much of Scotland, mainly in the north and west, and there are particular concentrations in Orkney, and to the north in Shetland. They comprise thick circular dry-stone walls, some of which reached a height of 13 metres, though it is likely that many were lower. On the outside they were windowless, with an austere tower-like appearance, but many were divided inside by stone partitions at ground floor level. The walls are hollow, with internal galleries rising from the ground or first floor, and it is likely that timber ranges opened from these to project out over part of the interior (in Orkney it has been suggested that stone may also have been used for some of the internal galleries). The whole must have been roofed with timber and thatch, but archaeologists are divided as to whether this roof covered the whole of the broch, or whether the central area was left open to the elements. Whatever, they must have been pretty dark inside.

In the past much has been written about the origins of the brochs, with archaeologists debating as to whether they were to be found earlier in the western or northern isles of Scotland. The arguments will, no doubt, continue to develop as more sites are excavated, and more information is brought to bear on the subject. In Orkney, the dates of some of the earliest sites, such as the Bu, show that the tradition of building robust, defended, circular structures goes back a long way to at least 600 BC. Brochs, it is argued, grew out of the needs of times that demanded both show and defence and thus people embellished their traditional circular houses. It seems that, here at least, it was a local development and not, as has sometimes been suggested, something that was brought in by travelling masons, similar to those who built the cathedrals of Scotland in the medieval period. Nevertheless, there are other structures that have been put forward as possible antecedents for the brochs in both Shetland and the Western Isles, and the situation is further complicated by the fact that broch structures are remarkably similar right across Scotland. There was certainly communication between different areas at the time, and perhaps the tradition arose from distinct structural beginnings in different places, as the response to similar times and needs was tempered by the movement of both people and ideas.

Only one broch survives almost intact: that at Mousa in Shetland, which reaches over 13 metres high. At the top there is a wall-walk which commands imposing views over the surrounding coastlands. Not all brochs necessarily stood to anything like this original height, but even lower brochs would still have had good views, and this, together with their general impregnable nature, and the presence on many sites of additional defences that include both ditches and ramparts, has led archaeologists in the past to interpret them as essentially defensive structures. This may have been so, but it is important not to lose sight of the fact that brochs were also dwellings, sometimes apparently for several families, and their imposing nature may well have had other significance.

General information on the Celtic society of the Iron Age period suggests that communities were led by strong individuals, leaders who were keen to show off their own wealth and exercise control over both the community and those who entered it. Many brochs lie in significant locations along routeways, and it is likely that they provided an element of regulation for those who occupied them. This was a time of increasing travel and transport; goods, both exotic and commonplace, were imported from the outside and the broch dwellers would certainly be well aware of those who made use of the local seaways and land routes. They may well have imposed local taxes. At the same time, an element of neighbourly conflict made it important both to defend your own goods and exercise the ability to steal your neighbours' possessions. Cattle were particularly vulnerable to this and the evidence suggests that they may well have been regarded as an important source of wealth. This neighbourly nit-picking and display is as likely to explain the nature of the brochs as any other reason, because there is little other evidence for major warfare in Orkney at the time. In this way, a broch would become an important symbol, indicating the status

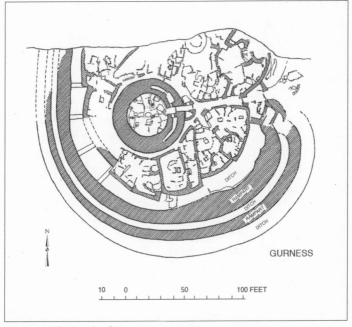

Figure 21. The broch of Gurness.

and authority of an individual community, as well as its strength and apparent inviolability. This was a time of developing hierarchy in society and the tower itself has been seen as a residence for the elite, while lesser mortals occupied the settlements clustered around their walls.

Inside, the broch was a sophisticated structure with a complex internal arrangement of slab-built features around a central hearth. These included various 'rooms' and cupboards or recesses. Many brochs contained internal wells and some had underground cellars. The broch would accommodate a substantial family, but it was often supplemented outside by settlements of stone houses that nestled up to the broch wall. At the Broch of Gurness on the Mainland side of Eynhallow Sound, these opened off a central street and they were carefully planned. Each house included a yard as well as a living area together with smaller partitioned spaces. There was a hearth and all the usual paraphernalia of other Iron Age structures: water tanks; cupboards; and recesses. The broch at Howe, outside Stromness, also included a substantial external settlement with many sophisticated structural features and both here and at Gurness these apparently included internal lavatories.

Domestic Life

The Iron Age communities of Orkney were farmers with cattle, sheep and goats, as well as pigs and dogs, but they also hunted and fished. Their architecture suggests that society was stratified into different levels and their artefacts show a rich economy with fine bone tools and pottery as well as rarer metal objects, including jewellery. There is some evidence that metal goods were made locally, for example at the Howe, where one of the buildings outside the broch was interpreted as a smithy. Communications outwith the islands continued to operate, and there are examples of Roman goods and other exotic objects that made their way to Orkney. Excavation of a newly-discovered broch at The Cairns in South Ronaldsay has provided increased detail of the domestic life of those who occupied the brochs.

The farmers of the Iron Age lived in a period of uncertainty, if not of major warfare. Some chose to live in the comparative security afforded by the settlements clustered around the brochs. Others lived outside, in apparently open, undefended settlements, such as the traces that were discovered to the east of Kirkwall around the earth-house at Grain. However, there are also other defended sites that do not include a broch, and these are the promontory forts, such as that at the Castle of Burwick in South Ronaldsay or the Brough of Bigging, near to Yesnaby in Mainland. The promontory forts did not incorporate a massive stone tower, but they did include substantial ramparts, which were used together with ditches to cut off the approaches to a settlement area. Promontory forts are relatively rare in Orkney, and as none has been excavated in modern times they are hard to date precisely, but they are a common feature of Iron Age times elsewhere in Scotland.

Another Iron Age site type commonly found elsewhere in Scotland comprises crannogs – roundhouses that are set on to a small, often artificial, island. Crannogs do exist in Orkney, most notably at Voy at the head of the loch of Stenness, and at Burrian, in the loch of Wasbister in Rousay. There has been little research, and no modern excavation of crannog sites in Orkney, however, so that the importance of this type of settlement is impossible to determine.

Earth-Houses

Besides the brochs and settlement structures of Iron Age Orkney, there is one other monument type related to this period, and it too seems to be domestic. This is the earth-house, an underground structure sometimes known elsewhere as a 'souterrain'. Earth-houses comprise long underground passages which lead to rounded chambers. They are generally completely stone lined, with stone roofs, and they were invisible from above ground. In the chamber the roof may be supported by various end-set slabs or pillars, and at the other end of the passage there were usually stone steps or a hatch leading up to the ground surface.

Earth-houses were generally associated with domestic buildings on the ground surface, and the entrance usually led down from inside a house. Some earth-houses, for example that at Grain outside Kirkwall, may have occurred in groups and were associated with traces of a larger settlement on the surface of the ground. One, excavated by Don Brothwell at Deerness in the east of Mainland, was a double structure. Unlike the broch settlements, the buildings from which earth-houses lead do not seem to have stood inside substantial stone and earth defences or enclosures, and they add to the evidence that people also lived in simple, unprotected round-houses at the time.

Recent excavations have taken place on several earth-houses, both for research, as at Windwick and The Cairns in South Ronald-say, and where they are accidentally discovered during farm work, as at Ness Breck in Harray. Some earth-houses, as at Windwick, were constructed in the later Bronze Age, while others are later. At The Cairns the earth-house postdates the broch.

Archaeologists usually interpret earth-houses as storage facilities, though there is often little evidence for the fillings that were associated with their original use. When they are excavated, domestic

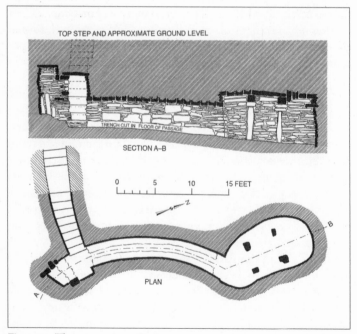

Figure 22. The souterrain at Grain.

84

midden refuse is the most common filling, though the earth-house at Rennibister, to the west of Kirkwall, contained the bones from at least eighteen people (six adults and twelve children), when it was first opened the 1920s. This is most unusual; no other earth-house burials have been found and it is likely that some individual prehistoric tragedy, and a secondary use of the earth-house, is represented here, rather than a general trend.

Burial and Ceremony

Iron Age burial in Orkney was, for a long time, a grey area for archaeologists. There are burials from this period elsewhere in Britain, but until recently evidence from Orkney was lacking. The excavation of Berstness in Westray has, however, changed this. The small skerry of Knowe of Skea lies just off the southern coast of Westray, and the site of Berstness comprises a complex of stone buildings dating as far back as 200 BC and set on the island. The principal structures here are clearly ceremonial and they were altered and rebuilt many times. Buried among and outside them the archaeologists discovered over 100 human skeletons, over 60 per cent of which were infants. Many of these remains lie among the rubble of the stone buildings and they look almost casual to the modern observer, but this was clearly a highly significant ritual centre for the Iron Age inhabitants of Westray.

Further evidence for Iron Age burial comes from the ceremonial site at Mine Howe in Tankerness, where two human skeletons were discovered among the remains of a large roundhouse associated with metalworking. Elsewhere, it is possible that cist burial, with or without a mound, may have continued from the Bronze Age. If so, it might well be difficult to distinguish it from earlier burials and much evidence may simply have disappeared amongst many of the 'explorations' of previous centuries.

Mine Howe is also important for the contribution it has made to knowledge of Iron Age ceremony. At the heart of the site lies a steep shaft that parallels the cellars and wells to be found within many brochs. This was set within a deep stone-lined ditch. There were other structures here, and there is abundant evidence for metalworking, both bronze and iron. The site was in use for a considerable period of time, and together with sites elsewhere in Scotland it seems to point to the importance of subterranean structures as a significant element of Iron Age ritual.

Later Iron Age Communities

Iron Age Orkney is dominated by the brochs, though, as has been seen, they are by no means the only monuments to survive from this period. Indeed, there is some indication that towards the end of the Iron Age many had fallen out of use and into disrepair. At the Howe the broch tower was allowed to collapse (some archaeologists have seen this as the result of a dramatic event) and the defences were abandoned. Some of the families from the previous defended village must have moved away, and a single undefended farmstead was built on the site. This farmstead was occupied around the fourth century AD. It consisted of various buildings, some of which are interpreted as sheds while others were for domestic use. Architectural styles had changed, and these buildings no longer reflected the traditional roundhouse of earlier times. The evidence from The Cairns also indicates that the broch structure was adapted, but not abandoned during the later Iron Age. Activities continued within cleared sections of the interior and at some stage dwelling structures were constructed both within and without the original tower, amidst the rubble that covered the site.

At Howe the evidence suggests that the community was much smaller at this time than that previously in the Iron Age. If this is a reflection of a general trend, then it would seem that people dispersed from the previous communal settlements to live in individual farmsteads dotted around the countryside. The lack of defences suggests that life had become more secure. Though there is little archaeological evidence for this move, other, more open settlements from this time have also been revealed by excavations at Skaill in Deerness and Pool in Sanday. Evidence from old excavations has also been reassessed to suggest that some sites, such as that at Howemae on North Ronaldsay, which was excavated in the 1880s, may have been occupied in the later Iron Age as farmsteads comprising both circular and rectangular buildings with interconnecting courtyards. The archaeological evidence may be obscure, but it is likely that the communities who lived in these new, dispersed farmsteads belonged to a new social order: the Picts, who are discussed in the next chapter.

Orkney and the Romans

Despite the apparently competitive nature of society that led to the building of impressive monuments such as the Iron Age brochs, there is little hard evidence for serious aggression in Orkney at the time. This was a period of upheaval elsewhere in Scotland, as the Romans extended their influence north, but it is hard to estimate the strength of the Roman threat to Orkney. A later writer, Eutropius, wrote that the Orcadian King submitted to the Roman emperor Claudius in AD 43, and the islands were clearly known about in the Roman Empire: Tacitus records that the emperor Agricola sent his fleet around Britain, and that during this trip the islands known as the Orcades were found and conquered. This took place about AD 80. There was clearly an awareness of Roman penetration further south, but Roman influences do not seem to have been of great impact in Orkney. Broch building had started earlier, and though they would clearly have been a useful defence, both symbolic and practical, against any seaborne foreigners such as Agricola's fleet, it is likely that these towers were primarily a local reaction to a local situation.

Occasional Roman artefacts did make their way north, to be used and later lost on local sites for future generations of archaeologists to find. The excavations at the Broch of Gurness uncovered a Roman amphora that would have been made between about 20 BC and AD 50. Items such as this may have been used to carry olives or sweet wine to the islands, while in the post-broch layers at the Howe a fine carnelian insert decorated with an engraving of an imperial eagle from a second-century finger ring was found. It is impossible to tell whether these goods represent direct contact with the Roman world, or whether they resulted from more indirect connections.

IRON AGE SITES (see map, p. xxix)

1 Mine Howe, Mainland   HY 511060

Private; signposted; small car park and exhibition.

The dominant structure at the heart of Mine Howe comprises the great mound with its central shaft, lined with stone stairs that dog-leg down towards a chamber. Around the outside of the mound a deep stone-lined ditch served to emphasise its prominence and also marked a boundary for the structures and activities that took place towards the edges of the complex. Access to the interior was provided by a narrow causeway, and the activities here included ironworking: a small furnace was discovered to one side of the enclosure. Outside, the ditch excavation has revealed a series of structures including a large roundhouse, apparently devoted to bronze working. Within the floor deposits of this structure lay the body of a young woman, dated to around 100 BC – 100 AD. This burial was carefully made and contrasted greatly with that of a young man, only feet away, outside the building. His burial was more casual and had been covered by rubble. The third burial from Mine Howe comprised that of a baby, interred in a stone setting within the top of the ditch and apparently late in the site's history.

Mine Howe was a complex site; activity here incorporated a variety of elements from metalworking to death. It may well have acted as a focus for communities across Orkney. Evidence for similar sites elsewhere is gradually coming to light, especially on the island of Skye, where the site at High Pasture Cave has many similarities to Mine Howe. Underground rituals clearly played an important role in Iron Age ceremony.

2 Broch of Gurness, Mainland   HY 381268

Historic Scotland; signposted; visitor centre and car park.

Most of the remains at Gurness date from the first millennium BC. The central broch tower is still impressive, though it is much denuded today; originally it may have reached a height of as much as 10 metres. It is surrounded by defences comprising three ditches with stone ramparts, and there are also the remains of a settlement of small stone houses arranged between the tower and the inner ditch. These were built after the broch tower, but they were clearly planned with the broch in mind, and it is likely that they were inhabited while it was still in use. Several of the houses open from a main street, which runs up to the entrance to the broch, and others from a passage which circles the broch. Each house is divided into several rooms and they also have hearths, yards and storage areas. The planning of the village included drainage and latrines.

Inside the broch tower various partitions and fittings from the later period of use may be seen, as well as a large central hearth and a well. Steps lead up into the wall, where there would have been galleries, possibly with a wooden range that projected out over the broch interior.

Activity at Gurness continued at least into the fifth century AD, when a series of smaller buildings were built over the ruins of the broch by Orcadian Picts, probably using the remains of the old settlement as a source for their stone. The remains of two of their houses are now preserved near to the visitor centre. Finally, a Norse woman was buried in the ruins, probably sometime in the ninth century AD. She was laid to rest in a stone-lined grave and given a pair of bronze brooches, an iron sickle, and an iron knife, as well as a necklet, to accompany her in the afterlife (her grave goods may now be seen in The Orkney Museum in Kirkwall).

From the Broch of Gurness one looks out across Eynhallow Sound to the island of Rousay. It seems that this was an important stretch of water bounded by fertile farmlands in the Iron Age. On either side of the Sound there are the remains of several broch towers, which attest to a numerous Iron Age population. Was it, perhaps, up here that Agricola's fleet sailed in AD 80, to be confronted by a series of tall and dominating broch towers? There are certainly Roman goods that have been discovered from some of the sites, though some, such as the amphora from Gurness, are earlier, and may have made their way to Orkney by other means.

There is a small visitor centre at Gurness with displays of artefacts from the site and information about life in Iron Age and Pictish times.

3 Broch of Borwick, Mainland   HY 224167

Private; cliff walk to site; care needed.

Although they are in a very ruinous state, the remains of the Broch
of Borwick are well worth visiting. The remaining part of the tower
stands to a height of about 3 metres, and it was probably built in
the mid-first millennium BC. It stands in a spectacular position on
the cliff top, and was originally protected by added defences to the

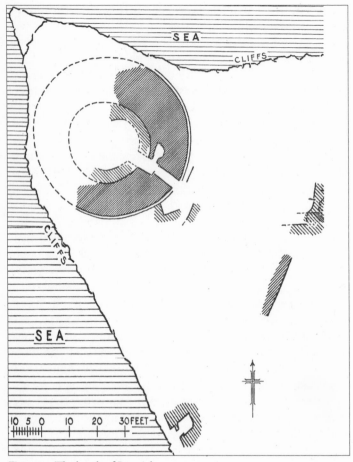

Figure 23. The broch of Borwick.

landward side. Today, the entrance and structure of the broch may still be clearly seen. Excavation in the last century showed that there had originally been some settlement around the broch and that the site continued in use into the first millennium AD. Borwick is a good place for a site such as this: it was naturally defended and clearly visible on the high cliff top; there is fresh water close by; and boats could be drawn up on the coast below. Some of the finds from the broch are in the Orkney Museum.

4 Oxtro Broch, Mainland   HY 254267

Private; at side of road.

Although most Orkney brochs have been excavated at some time, most are not laid out for display to the public. Oxtro gives a good idea of the appearance of these monuments as they occur in the countryside. All that is left today of the proud Iron Age tower is a low stony mound in the field between the modern road and the loch.

5 Broch of Midhowe, Rousay   HY 371306

Historic Scotland; signposted; footpath to site.

The broch tower at Midhowe survives to over 4 metres high, and was probably built towards the end of the first millennium BC. It lies in a naturally defensive position, built on a small promontory and cut off on either side by natural sea inlets that were joined by two deep ditches and a massive stone rampart. As at Gurness, the central tower was surrounded by a settlement of stone houses, each with its own yard, though here these seem to have been added and used later in the sequence of broch use.

Inside the broch tower there are the remains of a complex of stone partitions and fitments, though many of those to be seen today relate to later alterations in the internal arrangements. The interior is divided into two main rooms, each with a hearth, and there is a cellar or underground well in the northernmost room. As at Gurness the tower wall was hollow, with a first-floor gallery, but the builders of Midhowe had also incorporated an internal ground-floor gallery; this considerably weakened the structure of their building and in one area buttressing had to be added to the outside of the tower in order to prevent its collapse (at this point the lower gallery here was also filled with rubble, so it seems that the broch's inhabitants had a real problem on their hands). A wooden ladder originally led from the ground floor onto the wooden platform of the first-floor gallery, but this was later replaced by a stone stairway.

Midhowe was excavated in the 1930s, and much detail of everyday broch life was uncovered. This included not only ordinary goods, such as pottery and stone and bone tools, but also evidence for the on-site manufacture of metal artefacts, using both bronze and iron. In addition, there were a few Roman objects, mainly pottery, suggesting trade, or some sort of contact, with the peoples further south.

Midhowe lies on the north shore of Eynhallow Sound, almost opposite the Broch of Gurness. There are eleven brochs lining the

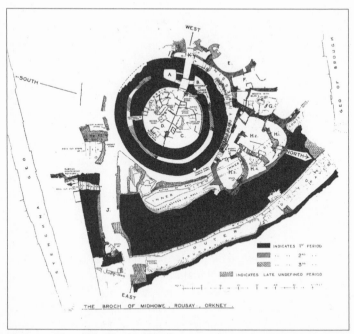

Figure 24. Plan of the broch of Midhowe.

northern and southern shores of the sound, suggesting that it may have been an important routeway in the Iron Age.

6 Burroughston Broch, Shapinsay
HY 541210

OIC.

The central broch tower was probably built in the second half of the first millennium BC, and was originally defended by a ditch with two ramparts which may have completely encircled it. The incursions of the sea, together with later building activity, have now destroyed much of the original structure. Nevertheless, it is still an imposing site, which has been restored to above the height of the

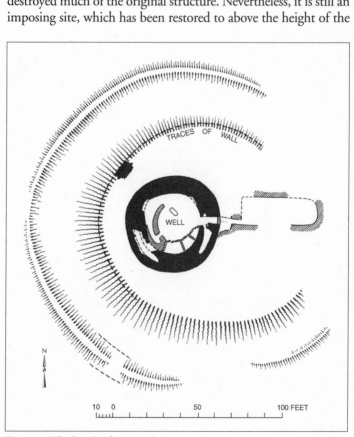

Figure 25. The broch of Burroughston.

first floor. The checks and bar-holes to secure the door may be seen in the entrance passage, as well as a guard cell that leads off it. Inside, there is a well and traces may be seen of the original divisions and fittings, but they are not as well preserved as at Gurness or Midhowe. Outside the broch the ground is grass-covered, but it is possible to make out the humps and bumps that mark the site of a settlement between the tower and its defences.

7 Lamb Ness Broch, Stronsay   HY 691214

Private; coastal walk to site.

Lamb Ness broch survives as a grassy covered mound in which traces of walling may be seen. It gives a good idea of the appearance of a broch before it has been laid out for public display, though it has been explored on several occasions and interior chambers are reported as well as a surviving entrance passage. In common with other brochs it is likely to have been built in the first millennium BC.

8 Broch of Burrian, North Ronaldsay   HY 762513

Private with access agreement; coastal walk to site.

This is an impressive broch with good outer defences, as well as traces of exterior settlement. It was probably built in the first millennium BC, but excavation in the last century revealed that there were also Pictish buildings and finds here from settlement in the fourth or fifth centuries AD, so activity at the Broch of Burrian continued long after the original broch tower must have gone out of use.

9 Castle of Burwick, South Ronaldsay   ND 434842

Private; walk from road; care needed on steep cliffs.

This is a rare Orcadian example of a first millennium BC fortified site that does not include a broch tower. The castle itself comprises a rocky peninsula joined to the mainland by a narrow neck of land and with steep, sheer drops on all sides. It is defended by four ramparts and ditches, and traces of grass-covered structures may be seen within the fort itself.

10 Brough of Bigging, Mainland   HY 218157

Private; coastal walk along high cliffs from Yesnaby; care needed.

The Brough of Bigging is another example of a fortified coastal site that did not comprise a broch. Here a high promontory was defended by two ramparts built across its neck.

11 Middle Banks, Stronsay   HY 689234

Private; care needed.

This is the remains of another promontory fort, possibly of Iron Age date. A stone wall about 2 metres thick cuts off the promontory, and traces of buildings may be made out behind it.

12 Grain Earth-house, Mainland   HY 441116

Historic Scotland; signposted; parking; key available nearby (currently the Ortak showroom); a torch is supplied, but it is useful to have one with you; not for the claustrophobic.

Grain is a deep earth-house, about 2 metres below the ground surface. Steps lead down into a narrow, low passage, which runs to an oval chamber with a stone roof supported on four stone pillars. Excavation work has uncovered a second, smaller earth-house close by, and there was other evidence of houses at ground level. The earth-houses were probably entered from inside a house and used for storage, and it is likely that they were in use in the first millennium BC.

13 Rennibister Earth-house, Mainland   HY 397125

Historic Scotland; signposted; park outside farmyard; a torch is supplied, but it is useful to have one with you.

This earth-house is now entered through a modern hatch and ladder that lead directly into the chamber. The passage that originally gave access is still visible, but it is narrow and low. The chamber had a corbelled roof, supported by four stone pillars, and there are various recesses and shelves in the walls. Rennibister was probably built sometime in the first millennium BC, to be used as storage from an Iron Age house above ground (the predecessor of the modern farm), but when it was discovered it contained the bones from at least eighteen people, including twelve children. There is no other evidence that earth-houses were used for burial, so it would seem that these remains represent a secondary use of the earth-house and relate to some unknown tragedy, probably in the Iron Age.

Rennibister was completely unknown until 1926, when a threshing machine in the farmyard above fell through the roof. Earth-houses, not surprisingly, may collapse and weaken the present ground surface, and when one is discovered in this way it is a reminder of just how many sites may yet await discovery.

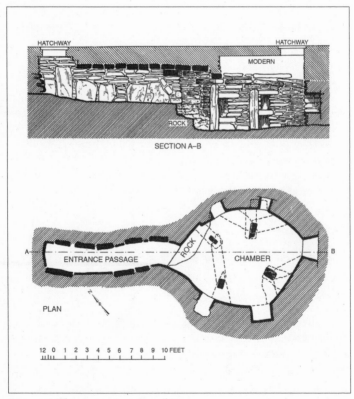

Figure 26. The souterrain at Rennibister.

Sea stack and cliffs at Yesnaby.

TOP. Part of the Neolithic farmstead at Knap of Howar.

ABOVE. One of the Skara Brae houses with Skaill House in the background.

TOP. House interior at Skara Brae.

ABOVE. Stone circle at Brodgar.

TOP LEFT. One of the standing stones at Brodgar.

TOP RIGHT. The Dwarfie Stane on Hoy.

ABOVE. Interior of the chambered tomb at Taversoe Tuick, Rousay.

TOP. This aerial shot of Ness of Brodgar illustrates the location of the site on the narrow peninsula that runs between the lochs of Stenness and Harray. In the past the landscape would have looked slightly different due to lower sea-levels. (Hugo Anderson-Whymark)

ABOVE. Structure 12 at Ness of Brodgar. (Hugo Anderson-Whymark)

TOP. An aerial view of the excavations at Ness of Brodgar.
(Hugo Anderson-Whymark)

ABOVE. Structure 1 at Ness of Brodgar. (Hugo Anderson-Whymark)

TOP. Burnt Mound and Bronze Age structure at
Liddle Farm, South Ronaldsay.

ABOVE. The broch at Gurness with surrounding structures.

TOP. Entrance way to the broch at Gurness.

ABOVE. Orkney Archaeological Trust excavations in the circular structure at Mine Howe. (Orkney Archaeological Trust)

ABOVE.
Orkney Archaeological Trust at work
excavating the ditch at Mine Howe.
(Orkney Archaeological Trust)

LEFT.
Chapel and remains at Deerness.

TOP. An early view of the Neolithic remains in the Maeshowe area.

ABOVE. The Farm Museum at Kirbuster.

Detail of the Farm Museum at Corrigall. Note the roof made of heather simmans laid on the flagstone.

St Magnus Cathedral, Kirkwall.

Churchill barrier with sunken blockship
in the background.

Statue of St George outside
the Italian chapel.

The Italian Chapel in Lamb Holm. Nissen huts form
the basis of this ornate building.

14 Linkataing, Eday   HY 553393

Private.

The remains of a large roundhouse, presumably of Iron Age date, may be seen. There is some indication of internal division, and a saddle quern lies in the interior.

15 Calf of Eday Prehistoric Settlement,   HY 579386
   Calf of Eday

Private; boats to the Calf of Eday may be arranged from Calfsound in Eday.

The extensive remains of a prehistoric settlement that has been identified as Iron Age lie on the slope above the Neolithic long cairn. The locations of at least one circular building and other structures may be made out within this.

The Coming of the Missionaries:
Pictish Orkney

The Origins of the Picts

The name 'Orkney' has Celtic roots, perhaps suggesting a tribe with the boar or young pig as its totem. It was used by Irish historians to refer to the islands and occurs in a first-century account made by one Dioderus Siculus, taken from a fourth-century Greek voyager, Pytheas. Orkney was certainly known to the Romans and it is mentioned by various classical authors, including Ptolemy and Tacitus. The former marked it on a map; the latter recounted the circumnavigation of northern Scotland by Agricola's fleet *c.* AD 80, but he gives little detail of the islands. By this time, however, Orkney was clearly considered worthy of inclusion in the general historical documents, even if only as an indication of far-off places.

The documentary references are rarely very detailed, and they are all open to differing interpretations, but it is clear that by the fourth century AD a new political configuration of peoples had arisen in Scotland: the Picts. The Pictish peoples developed from the local Iron Age Celtic tribes who had been forceful in previous centuries, and their territories were concentrated to the north of the Forth and Clyde rivers. The name 'Pict' implies that they may have used body paint or tattoos, and this, amongst other things, seems to have differentiated them from other peoples living elsewhere in Scotland. The Pictish 'nation' comprised several federations, each with its own leaders or kings, but for much time the centre of Pictish power lay on the Scottish mainland, to the south of Orkney, near to Inverness. Orkney, it seems, was a powerful part of Pictland, with its own kings.

Pictish Society

The Picts have long been considered to be an enigmatic people archaeologically. In some ways, much is known about them: they are cited in a range of writings; they produced fine metalwork and wonderful sculpture; there are Pictish inscriptions; and excavation is revealing increasing evidence for rich, sophisticated centres of power. However, in other ways the record is still lacking: many inscriptions cannot be read; recent research is changing this, but those that have so far been interpreted are short and tell us little about the people); the significance of the rich pagan sculptural symbolism is unknown; few ordinary domestic settlements have been excavated; little is known of their everyday material culture; and burial sites are rare. Nevertheless, the Pictish culture was dominant in Orkney for at least four centuries, and enough is known to indicate that during this time some very important changes came about.

Pictish society was clearly highly organised and hierarchical. The people spoke a form of Celtic (P-Celtic) which was related to other Celtic languages, such as the Welsh and the Gaulish languages, and was probably understood fairly widely through Britain. Orkney seems to have been a kingdom in its own right with its own Pictish king, but the main Pictish power bases lay south of Orkney. The evidence of both metalwork and sculpture indicates that warfare was an important part of Pictish life and from time to time the annals record aggression between Orkney and the other Pictish kingdoms further south. Not surprisingly in a country like Scotland, the Pictish forces were sea-based as well as land-based. In AD 681 it is recorded that King Bridei 'devastated' Orkney (though the precise nature of this destruction is a matter of academic debate). Orkney was also involved in its own right in warfare with Ulster and the Ulster Scots who were settling as the people of Dal Riada in Argyll in the west of Scotland. For the first time we can see the 'Orkneymen' acting as a unit and venturing forth under one leader.

About AD 565 St Columba visited the Pictish King Bridei mac Maelchon at his court near to Inverness, and met the Orkney king who was subservient to the main court. Columba was concerned about the safety of one of his hermits, who was looking for a site to settle in the north, and it is recorded that he asked Bridei to command the Orcadian king to ensure the hermit's well-being in

Orkney. Thus we have one of the first references to one of the major changes of these times: Christianity had arrived in the islands.

Christianity comes to Orkney

The events behind the establishment of the Church in Orkney are not recorded, but it is at this time that the first material goods relating to Christianity appear, and other documentary references, mixed with legend, also refer to religious matters. St Columba's hermit was probably not the first Christian to visit the islands, nor was he the only one at the time. Various early Christian sites have been identified in Orkney, including many early church dedications to St Peter throughout the islands, as well as some isolated hermitage sites along the rocky coastline. It is suggested that an early bishop had his seat at St Boniface in Papa Westray; nearby is a later chapel dedicated to St Tredwell, who was associated with St Boniface, and it seems that the island was of some importance at this time.

On the small tidal island of Birsay, just off the north-west coast of Mainland, lay an important centre of Norse Christianity. This is underlain by Pictish remains which may have included a religious foundation, though little is known about them. The structural remains of Pictish settlement in Birsay were very fragmentary, but the other finds were enough to suggest that the community here was wealthy. The Pictish horizon at Birsay included much evidence of metalworking, in particular fine pieces of jewellery: brooches; pins; and finger rings. Elsewhere in Pictland, this sort of specialised activity seems to have been confined to power centres where leaders not only had the resources to acquire the raw materials and pay the skilled craftsmen necessary to do the work, but also the status to use such high-class goods and affirm their authority. Archaeologists are generally agreed that Pictish Birsay must have been a centre of power.

Also at Birsay, a fine carved slab was discovered, now preserved by the National Museums of Scotland in Edinburgh, though a cast still stands on site. The stone shows three bearded warriors armed with spears and shields as well as some of the more enigmatic early Pictish designs, both naturalistic and stylised. The elaborate detail shows clearly the higher status of the leading figure and perhaps here there is a glimpse of one of the wealthy leaders who made use of the elaborate jewellery made at Birsay. Today the stone is fragmentary and there are various suggestions as to its interpretation: that it was originally part of a gravestone (its present position is rather misleading), or perhaps a cross slab. In effect there is no evidence for either explanation, though archaeologists think that the community in Birsay may well have included a religious centre.

Elsewhere in Orkney, in Flotta, the evidence was more unequivocal: the decorated front panel from a stone altar that dates to this period was discovered here and it is now with the National Museums of Scotland. Flotta clearly had a church in Pictish times and the fineness of its altar slab gives a hint of the sophistication and richness of the other churches that may have been scattered through the islands. Another cross slab was discovered in the nineteenth century within the remains of a ruined chapel at Osmundwall in South Walls. Recent related finds include a fragment of an elaborately carved cross slab, which was discovered beneath a stone floor in the island of Sanday. Finds such as these indicate the degree to which the Early Christian community of Pictish Orkney was a flourishing part of island life.

Material Culture

Today, the Picts are best known for their sculpture. Slabs carved with enigmatic symbols have been recovered from sites all over Pictland and more are still coming to light. The symbols include both naturalistic designs – birds, fish and animals – and more stylised elements such as rods and crescents. The same symbols, carved in very similar fashion, occur throughout Pictland, and there have been many attempts to interpret them. The Pictish sculptors were clearly working to a recognised pattern book, but its meaning remains unintelligible to us today (though many theories have been put forward by individual workers, for example that the symbols represent personal or family names; totemic lineages; elements of a language; or are indications of status or profession). The later symbol stones are easier to understand because they incorporate Christian and other motifs, and gradually the original designs were dropped from the suite of figures. The Birsay Stone is the most well-known Pictish stone from Orkney, but there are plenty of other examples of Pictish art here, and the Birsay Stone is, in fact, quite unlike any other.

Fine metal goods are another of the main strands of evidence for the Picts. Throughout their territory distinctive artefacts have been found, including heavy jewellery, bowls and sword fittings. Many objects are decorated, often using similar patterns to those that appear on the sculptured stones. Objects occur both singly and in hoards; the most famous hoard is that from St Ninian's Isle on the west coast of Shetland. This hoard included both domestic artefacts and fittings for weaponry. It had been buried beneath the floor of an early church, but was probably secular in origin. The St Ninian's Isle hoard is dated to about AD 800, at the end of the Pictish period in the Northern Isles, and it has been speculated that it was the property of a wealthy islander who was hiding it from the new threat posed by Norse raiders. Research by Dr James Graham-Campbell on a lost hoard of silver objects from the Broch of Burgar in Orkney has suggested that it too may have been a Pictish hoard, also buried towards the end of the Pictish period by a wealthy Orcadian Pict in an attempt to conceal it from Norse raiders. More commonplace Pictish objects included earthenware pottery, artefacts of bone and antler (including fine decorated combs), and occasional metal goods. Stone spindle whorls provide evidence for spun cloth.

The Settlement Evidence

Several Pictish houses were revealed by the excavations at Birsay, but they were fragmentary, with little detail. Nearby, at Buckquoy in Mainland, a sequence of Pictish settlements (now gone) was excavated by Anna Ritchie, and this has helped to provide much of our knowledge of domestic buildings at the time (the finds are in the Orkney Museum). The earlier phases at Buckquoy comprised cellular structures in which a series of small cells surrounded a central chamber with a hearth. In the final, third phase the house was completely redesigned and comprised a long stone-walled structure with a sunken chamber at one end. The main room contained a large, stone-lined hearth, and a pair of smaller rooms lay beyond.

This style of house is known as a 'figure-of-eight' house and both cellular and figure-of-eight houses have been excavated elsewhere in Pictland.

The settlement at Buckquoy has been interpreted as a farmstead; the evidence suggested that the inhabitants grew oats and bere barley, they kept cattle and sheep, and also fished. Their material goods included pottery, bone tools and jewellery, and a painted 'charm stone' was found on the site, but they kept their houses very clean and so few everyday goods were recovered. On the other side of Mainland, at Skaill in Deerness, a rather more substantial type of Pictish building has been excavated and this has been interpreted by the excavator as a more prestigious residence whose inhabitants had access to slightly more luxurious goods than the Buckquoy farmers.

Elsewhere in Orkney, evidence for Pictish settlement has been recovered mainly as a part of excavation on multi-period sites. The reduction in the defensive nature of some of the brochs at this time has been mentioned in the previous chapter. As the central broch tower went out of use, farmsteads comprising various structures of different types, including cellular or figure-of-eight houses, often sprang up around their base or in the rubble of the old broch tower. Evidence for this was uncovered during the excavations at Howe, near to Stromness, and may also be seen at Gurness. The excavations at The Cairns indicate a Pictish settlement in the later phases of the site and Pictish settlement remains underlay the Norse remains at Pool in Sanday. Most settlement at this time seems to have comprised individual farmsteads, rather than villages. Increasing rural settlement means that many Pictish houses may yet await discovery under more recently occupied sites.

Burial

The Pictish Orcadians were essentially a society that developed out of the later Iron Age communities. They lived in dispersed settlements of which little evidence survives today. Towards the end of the period they paid their respects to the local church, and their society included skilled artists and metalsmiths as well as a richer stratum and a local aristocracy. They were fighters and seamen, as well as peaceable farmers. Where were they buried? From evidence elsewhere in Scotland it seems that the Picts were generally buried without grave goods, sometimes in barrows surrounded by shallow ditches and later on in long stone cists. This means that it can be hard to distinguish their graves from those of other peoples. Evidence from Pictish Orkney is rare, but there are hints.

The presence of a sculptured stone on the Brough of Birsay suggests that some of the burials below the Norse remains may be of Picts, and in Mainland opposite Birsay a long cist inhumation was found close to the farmstead at Buckquoy. Close by, there is a mound, Saevarhowe, which contained long cist burials, perhaps of both Pictish and Norse date. In some places the long cists were covered by a low cairn with a surrounding kerb, and one of these was also identified at Buckquoy. Several Pictish burials, suggesting a cemetery site, were discovered during the excavation of later material at Westness in Rousay; and at Oxtro the broch was overlain by short cist burials, one of which had a Pictish symbol stone as its capstone. As ever, the picture is never simple. No doubt, many Pictish burials have been lost in the scramble to explore ancient sites that took place in the past; no doubt, many more still await discovery.

New finds do occur. During work to prepare Skaill House, near to Skara Brae, for visitors in the 1990s, human remains were uncovered in the course of digging a new drainage system around the house. Further archaeological work was undertaken by a team from Glasgow University and in all twelve skeletons were uncovered as well as several stone slabs. The remains clearly indicate the presence of a cemetery, and the type of burial suggests that this dates to the early Christian Pictish period. This cemetery was apparently completely unknown, though other skeletons had been uncovered during work on the house in the 1930s. Interestingly, the archaeologists also uncovered a stretch of early walling. It was not possible to establish whether this was of the same age as the skeletons, but the archaeologists have suggested that it could, perhaps, relate to a chapel contemporary with the burials.

PICTISH SITES (see map, p. xxix)

1 The Broch of Gurness, Mainland   HY 381268

Historic Scotland; signposted; visitor centre and car park.

A Pictish farmstead was built at the Broch of Gurness, long after
the original tower had gone out of use. The Pictish inhabitants of
the site made use of stone from the abandoned broch. The lower
courses of a small cellular house from this time have been moved
and rebuilt by the visitor centre, at the entrance to the site. Finds
from the settlement included some simple jewellery, as well as a
bone-handled metal knife and a stone with Pictish symbols.

The visitor centre includes displays relating to Pictish times.

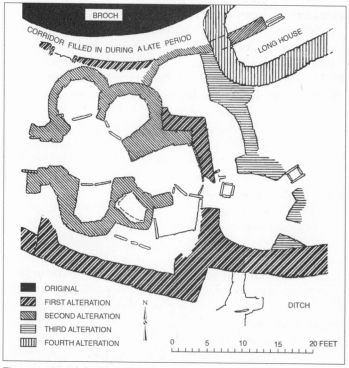

Figure 27. Pictish building built over earlier remains outside the broch of
Gurness.

2 Brough of Birsay, Mainland   HY 239285

Historic Scotland; signposted; car park; causeway at low tide; care needed.

Below the remains of an extensive Norse settlement and church there were the remains of a Pictish settlement and chapel. There were also graves below those of Norse times in the graveyard, and these are likely to have been Pictish. In the area of the graveyard lay the fragments of a symbol stone, now repaired and housed in the National Museums of Scotland in Edinburgh, but a cast has been placed on site. The stone combined the traditional Pictish symbols with three warriors incised on its lower half. The three appear to form some sort of procession and much detail is preserved: the leader (with long curly hair) has a finely decorated shield and a fringed tunic while his two followers have simpler shields and clothing; all carry spears and have sword scabbards.

A shallow well, still visible, supplied the settlement with fresh water, and excavations in the 1930s and 1950s uncovered many Pictish artefacts from the site, including much debris from metal-working. Though little evidence for Pictish houses has been found on the Brough of Birsay, it seems likely that there was a settlement of some importance here. Elsewhere in Pictland artefacts such as those uncovered from Birsay are associated with substantial, often high-status, sites. It has been suggested that the Pictish houses on Birsay were built of wood, thus accounting for the lack of evidence relating to them.

3 Skaill House, Sandwick, Mainland   HY 234186

Signposted; car park; a joint ticket is available with Skara Brae.

Skaill House itself dates back to the early seventeenth century, but in 1996, during work to open the house to visitors, evidence for earlier, Pictish, antecedents was found. Excavations uncovered a number of skeletons dating to Pictish times and it is thought likely that they relate to other skeletons recorded during work on the house in the 1930s. It is likely that there was a Pictish cemetery here, long before the house was built, and presumably a Pictish settlement lay close by, though no trace of this has yet been found.

Today, Skaill House is open to the visitor and it contains exhibitions illustrating various aspects of the history of the Bay of Skaill.

4 Brough of Deerness   HY 596087

OIC; signposted; car park; steep, rocky footpath best accessible at low tide; care needed.

The Brough of Deerness is known for its Norse remains, but recent excavations demonstrate that there was an earlier Pictish settlement here. While no sign of specifically Pictish dwellings remains on the surface of the ground, the later houses made use of their ruins and abundant traces of midden have been discovered. Whether this suggests continuity of settlement or a hiatus in the occupation of the impressive stack site remains to be clarified. We do not, therefore, know how or why the Pictish settlement ended, but it is clear that the Brough of Deerness was home to a substantial Pictish community.

5 St Boniface Church, Papa Westray   HY 488527
OIC.

St Boniface is essentially a twelfth-century church, though it has been much altered and extended and a private burial enclosure built in the chancel. It has Pictish connections, however: St Boniface is associated with the introduction of Christianity to the Picts and it has been suggested that Papa Westray was the seat of the Pictish bishopric of Orkney. Recent excavations have uncovered evidence for Pictish settlement in the vicinity, and the Norse gave the name 'Papa', meaning monks, to the island, suggesting that there was already a religious community there when they arrived. Furthermore, two early Christian cross slabs were discovered here earlier this century, one of which may now be seen in the Orkney Museum in Kirkwall, while the other is with the National Museums of Scotland in Edinburgh. These crosses add weight to the suggestion that St Boniface was an early foundation of some importance.

Near to St Boniface Church is a later chapel dedicated to St Tredwell, another early saint who was associated with St Boniface, and so it seems that the island was an active centre in Early Christian times.

Foreign Settlers:
The Norse in Orkney

The Arrival of the Norse

The Picts were seafarers and sallied forth from the islands on both peaceful and aggressive missions. Warriors and battle scenes appear on many of their carvings, and there is evidence that warfare came to be a fundamental element of life. St Columba was worried about the safety of a hermit journeying to the north and it seems that the Pictish kings often took power in an aggressive struggle and then fought to maintain it. The Pictish king of Orkney was powerful at home in the islands, but further afield he was apparently subservient to the king in Inverness, and in AD 565 the Orcadians at the court of Bridei in Inverness are described as hostages. Yet, in Orkney, the settlement evidence from this time indicates that the old broch defences were allowed to fall into disrepair, and that people moved away from the safety of the villages to individual farmsteads in the countryside. There seems to have been some stability for the common people, even in a time of political aggression and uncertainty.

Nevertheless, by AD 800, there are signs that things were changing. Elsewhere in Britain the records note the advent of a new, seaborne enemy: in AD 793 Norsemen raided Lindisfarne in Northumbria, and other raids are known. It has been suggested that some of these raids on the British mainland were carried out from newly established bases in the northern isles rather than from home territories in Scandinavia, and certainly they are a sign of the extension of Norse influence into the British Isles. Of course, raiding may also have been directed at the existing island communities and one interpretation of the St Ninian's Isle treasure in Shetland sees it as being buried in response to such a raid. A hoard of silver objects discovered at the Broch of Burgar in Orkney in 1840 (and subsequently lost again) may also have been buried to preserve it from falling into Norse hands. The aggressive intentions and locations of the home settlements of the Norse raiders are currently a matter of some debate between academics, but whether they were peaceable farmers looking for new lands, or violent thugs looking for bases from which to seek out treasure, the end result was the same: the Orcadian Picts had to cope with new island neighbours.

Today, Orkney is well known for its Scandinavian heritage, but the exact mechanisms by which the Norsemen became established in the islands are unclear. Norwegian settlement was expanding in the ninth century, and tradition and the sagas tell us that the Norwegian King Harald Finehair gifted the islands to the family of Earl Sigurd towards the end of the ninth century, after quelling troublesome Vikings who had already settled there. The accuracy of this story is disputed by many academics, but it is interesting because it indicates that by the ninth century Orkney already had a Norse population (if a disruptive one), and this is supported by other traditions as well as by the archaeological evidence.

Orkney had much to offer the seafarers of the Norse world: the gentle topography offered easy landings and good winter harbours; the land was fertile; and it provided a central maritime location. Given the rapid growth of the Norse empire it is not surprising that these assets were recognised early on by both the common populace and the powers-that-be.

The Picts and the Norse

What about relations between the Norse incomers and the old Pictish families? Here too the evidence is open to debate. The Norsemen clearly considered one important stretch of water in terms of their foreign neighbours: the name Pentland Firth is derived from *pettlands fjordr*, which means 'Pictland's firth', but the sagas give little detail about the subjugation of the local population, though some researchers have suggested that straightforward conquest was involved.

On the basis of the archaeological evidence, others suggest that Norsemen and Picts lived relatively peaceably together and that with time the Picts gradually became absorbed into the Norse population. The truth is probably a mixture of the two, but we shall never know for sure. In the past, it has been suggested that quite different Norse house styles and goods can be shown to replace the old Pictish dwellings on several sites, e.g. at Buckquoy in Birsay, but in other places the two house styles appear to have been more similar and at first the material goods of the people often retain the traditional 'Pictish' styles, suggesting a more gradual blending of the two cultures.

New Strands of Evidence

Much archaeological work has taken place to reveal detail of the Norse in Orkney, but new strands of evidence now come into play. The picture is supplemented by a rich store of detail from the sagas. The precise truth of these great traditional histories is questionable; they were oral stories for many decades before they were written down. Nevertheless, the Norse period in Orkney is unique in that for the first time, not only do we have the archaeological remains that dot the landscape, but we also have the names, and often descriptions, of the people who built and used them as well as unique information about the politics and various domestic events of the time. Of course in many cases specific archaeological sites do not figure in the sagas, and at the same time places that were written about have yet to be identified on the ground, but the combination of saga writing with archaeology has given Norse Orkney a very personal touch.

There is another element of evidence relating to Norse period Orkney, and that is the placenames. As the Norse incomers settled, they named their dwelling sites and other places of importance; as they expanded out across the islands, they named new settlements. Such was their influence that, while most of the old Pictish and earlier names have long been forgotten, a whole network of Norse names relating not only to homesteads but also to landmarks, and the local systems of administration and land taxes, is still current, if now corrupted and little understood in everyday terms. Thus, names such as 'the Bu' derive from the locations of large farms, while names incorporating 'garth' reflect the subdivision of land and creation of a new settlement. The analysis of the placename evidence is a very specialised subject, and it has added much detail to our knowledge about Norse society, its workings and how the landscape was perceived and used.

The Orkneyinga Saga

In addition to being mentioned in many of the sagas, Orkney is privileged in that one specific saga was devoted to the political history of the archipelago: the Orkneyinga Saga. This is well worth reading for a personal and highly colourful account of the events and main personalities of the day. The Orkneyinga Saga was compiled in Iceland in the late twelfth century from earlier oral histories and, while some of its chapters, such as those relating to the coming of the Norse to Orkney, may contain more story than fact, others cover events that can be historically documented. Many of the people who play a role in the saga can be identified with historical figures and many of the places where events took place can still be visited today. By this means it is possible to name and describe some of those who actually lived within some of the sites that have been excavated: a rare chance for the modern archaeologist.

Norse Politics

The sagas give a unique insight into the local and national politics of the Norse earls in Orkney, but this was a complicated business for there was much inter-rivalry and constant changes of power within the various main families. The politics of the Norse kingdom, and of Orkney as an earldom within that kingdom, are difficult to unravel, but it is clear that Orkney was an important element of the Norse world. It was the first earldom to be created subject to the Norwegian kings, and it occupied a vital strategic position in both economic and military terms.

The earls of Orkney were important figures who worked hard to extend their power outwith their island home among the western Norse colonies. Geographically, Orkney was well placed for boats undertaking the sea crossing between Scandinavia and the isles of Britain and Ireland, it offered sheltered harbours and was much visited both by royal and other expeditions as a secure stopping-off point before and after excursions into the territories further south and west. This served to enhance relations between the Orca-dian earls and their Scandinavian overlords and colleagues. At the same time relations were secured, sometimes by marriage and at other times through violence with neighbouring native earls, such as those of Caithness. In this way the early earls played an important role in the spread and consolidation of Scandinavian power and influence throughout the British Isles.

The influence of the Orcadian earls culminated in 1014 when Earl Sigurd, whose mother was an Irish princess, gathered a force of men from as far afield as Brittany, the Isle of Man and Kintyre, Argyll and the Western Isles, to join with Orcadians and Shetlanders in an alliance with Irish Norsemen under King Sitric of Dublin. Their aim was to fight in Ireland to reduce the power of the Irish King Brian Boru, who was extending his influence and authority among the former Norse territories. The resulting battle, the Battle of Clontarf, is well known from contemporary records. The Norse-men were fighting to protect their coastal trading routes and centres from increasing domination by the Irish and their defeat at the battle is generally held to represent the end of an era; even at the time it was recognised as an event of far-reaching importance. Sigurd himself died in the battle; his death had been foretold and he is said to have died with his banner, with its famous raven motif, wrapped around him. Sigurd's death passed quickly into the annals of folk history and with him died the ideals of the spread of Norse-Orcadian power. Future earls would be more modest and inward-looking in their ambitions for political success.

Earl Sigurd's political ambitions had aimed to extend Norse-Orcadian power south and west outside the islands of his home. His second wife was the daughter of the King of the Scots, and with this union he set the path for the increasing importance of Scottish links with Orkney. The son of this marriage, Earl Thorfinn, grew up in his grandfather's court in Scotland and was a good example of the dual political influences at play. He ultimately came into power in Orkney (after conflict with his three half-brothers who ruled there after their father's death), and visited the Norwegian court for political reasons on several occasions, but it is also recorded that he maintained strong links with the Scots. Thorfinn recognised the authority of the Norwegian King, but his power extended over the lands of Caithness which had originally been in native Scottish hands, and he may have allied with the Scottish royal family and participated in their struggle to maintain power further south. He even joined in raids on England, bringing his men from Orkney, in 1042.

Thorfinn died about 1065 and at this time the Scandinavian world began to drift apart. Farther south, in England, the sons of Thorfinn fought with Harald Hardrada and were defeated at the battle of Stamford Bridge. No doubt they had Orcadians with them. Subsequent to this battle the English troops were themselves defeated at Hastings by the Normans under William: new political powers were beginning to emerge.

Life in Orkney continued in an essentially Scandinavian vein, but in 1138 there succeeded to the earldom a five-year-old boy who was to play an important part in the increasing hold of Scotland over the islands. This earl was Harald Maddadsson, who was descended from both the Norwegian and the Scottish aristocracies and has been described as one of the great earls of Orkney. Harald was born in Scotland, but he grew up in Orkney and throughout his life he was torn between allegiance to the Norwegian and the Scottish crowns. Even his married life was affected by this struggle: his first wife was the daughter of a Scottish noble, the Earl of Fife, but he made a second marriage, apparently initially for political reasons, to the daughter of a rebel Scot who backed the Norwegian cause (the marriage may have turned into a love match: later on he was asked to give up his second wife in favour of the first, but he refused).

Harald split control of the earldom of Orkney with Earl Rognvald, the founder of St Magnus Cathedral, who had also recently come to power. Although he was at first supported by the Scottish crown, by the time he was 18 he was paying allegiance to the then king of Norway, King Eystein. For the rest of his life he would have to balance the counter-claims of the Scottish and Norwegian courts. Both were facing a series of problems with rebels, and Harald seems to have had a knack for choosing the losing side: this was to have important consequences for Orkney. In the 1180s he sided with the MacWilliam family, who had mounted an unsuccessful challenge to the Scottish throne in the north. By the 1190s, however, his eye had turned to Norway and in 1192 he backed a rival to the Norwegian throne in a rebellion that was also to be defeated. As a result he had to renew his fealty to the Norwegian king, but his attention then turned back to Scotland where the Scottish king, William the Lion, was consolidating his power with a series of military expeditions, one of which came north to Thurso in 1196. Earl Harald was forced to make terms with him, but in 1197 he was taken prisoner and held in Edinburgh until his son could be brought to take his place. At this time there was also a rival claim for power at home in Orkney, backed by the Norwegian king, though this was defeated by Harald. Harald had, by now, been in power for many years, but he was caught up into the web of politics at the time and his relationship with both the Scottish and the Norwegian crowns remained troubled until his death in 1206.

Norse control of the islands continued until 1231, when Earl John was killed in a drunken brawl in Thurso. By this time Scottish influence over the local aristocracy was such that with the death of Earl John it was the Scottish earls of Angus who inherited the earldom.

Society and Domestic Life

Norse society was highly stratified and included various social levels from the aristocracy downwards through free farmers to thralls with no legal rights. With regard to the common people and their way of life, much of our information comes from archaeological work. In style most of the later Norse homes were very different from the preceding Pictish houses. Long rectangular buildings, sometimes with rounded ends, were built of stone, or turf and stone, with internal hearths and fittings such as benches. There were various outbuildings to house animals, equipment and stores, and the archaeological evidence suggests that homesteads were frequently rebuilt. Recent excavations have added a wealth of environmental evidence to the picture so that there is now more detail of the crops and animals that were the mainstay of the farming settlements. Barley and oats were common, and cattle, sheep and pigs were kept, though meat supplies were supplemented by fish and also seabirds. Norse farmers were very self-sufficient.

The settlement evidence comprises mainly individual farmsteads, though there were a few larger villages. Steadings varied in size and status, from humble dwellings to great hall house complexes that housed the wealthy aristocracy and their followers. At Snusgar, to the north end of the Bay of Skaill in Sandwick, David Griffiths of Oxford University has excavated a dwelling of some status. In an attempt to shed light on the context of the fine Viking Skaill hoard of silver objects, which was discovered in this area in the mid-nineteenth century, the team have uncovered the remains of a large stone longhouse and associated outbuildings dating to the tenth and eleventh centuries. Many high-quality finds indicate that this was a site of some significance.

On the other side of Mainland, James Barrett and his team from the McDonald Institute for Archaeological Research in Cambridge have been excavating at the Brough of Deerness, to investigate the Viking remains on the sea stack. He reinterprets this site as the high-status centre of a local chief. Occupation of the stack started in the Pictish period, and by Viking times there were several well-built longhouses from which a rich array of finds has been recovered. Settlement focused around a small chapel, indicating that Christianity was important, but it is no longer thought to have been an ecclesiastical community as once suggested. There

Figure 28. A nineteenth-century view of the Brough of Deerness.

is no record in the sagas of the settlement at Deerness, but it is well placed, both as a defensive site and as a point of control, to keep an eye on those who might approach Orkney from the east.

Archaeology has provided much detail of the raw materials of the lifestyle of the Norse inhabitants of Orkney and it is filled out by the sagas, which give vivid descriptions of the life, and domestic and political intrigue, that went on in and around them. While people lived and farmed on the fertile islands it was the sea that provided the focal point of society. Water can be a unifying power as well as a barrier and in Norse times it was from across the sea that political power was maintained and from here came many goods, both familiar and exotic. Orkney is well placed to be the centre of a maritime culture, and boats, whether grand longships or small skiffs, were a vital part of life for everyone. Elsewhere in the Scandinavian world archaeological discoveries have led to a wealth of information about the different types of boat used by the Norsemen and the sophisticated technology that was associated with them. From Orkney there has been little physical evidence of actual ships, though there is some information from boat burials such as those of Scar, in Sanday, and Westness, in Rousay, but round the coasts of Orkney lie many 'nousts': shelters, often built of stone, into which both longships and smaller vessels could be drawn for protection over the rough winter months.

Religion

The Norse Orcadians were a religious people. After the Pictish period, Christianity in the islands seems to have waned: there is a saga which tells of the forced conversion of Earl Sigurd and his followers, in the late tenth century, aboard the boat of his rival Olaf Trygvesson in the bay of Osmundwall in the south of Hoy. The placename evidence suggests that some Christian communities did survive during the early Norse period: islands incorporating the element Papa, as in Papa Westray, for example, have been suggested as the location of priestly settlements, but other evidence, including that from burials and various documents, indicates that Christianity had lapsed in most places. Nevertheless, the pagan Norsemen would certainly have had contact with neighbouring Christian societies and it is likely that Sigurd's mother and wife were Christian, though it was apparently only after his own acceptance of the religion that Christianity became generally established within Orkney. There is still, however, some academic debate as to how much the establishment of Christianity in the isles was actually consequent on Earl Sigurd's conversion.

Whatever the date, or origin, of the establishment of Christianity in Orkney, once it was generally accepted it seems to have spread quickly and the Norse Orcadians were responsible for building many churches and chapels throughout the islands. Research suggests that it was at this time that the present parish system was founded. The Church in Orkney worked hard to undermine the old pagan religion, and this has, of course, affected surviving information about the earlier beliefs and practices. There is, however, a wealth of material relating to Christian sites. Religious centres are referred to in the texts and the remains of several churches and chapels may still be visited. One of the best-known sites is on the Brough of Birsay, where the foundations of a stone church lie surrounded by a substantial settlement that probably included both ecclesiastical and secular buildings. On the mainland opposite stood an important church, known as the Christchurch, built by Sigurd's son, Earl Thorfinn, who had journeyed on a pilgrimage to Rome and had had an audience with the Pope in about 1050. Thorfinn established the bishopric of Orkney, and archaeologists have suggested that the remains of his minster, the Christchurch, lie under the present kirk at Birsay, but this has yet to be verified.

Figure 29. A view of the remains in Eynhallow in the nineteenth century.

It is likely that the settlement in the Brough of Birsay included monks, and there were other monastic sites in the islands. The name of the island of Eynhallow is derived from the Old Norse 'Eyin Helga', meaning Holy Isle, and here too are the remains of a twelfth-century church, which the sagas tell us was the centre of a Norse monastery and which possibly had earlier foundations.

St Magnus

In about AD 1115 there occurred an event which was to help to change the face of church building in Orkney. This was the murder, or martyrdom, of Earl Magnus Erlendsson by his rival for control of the islands, Earl Hakon Paulsson. It took place in the tiny island of Egilsay, where they had met to settle their differences. Magnus already had a reputation for sanctity, preferring to read holy psalms rather than join in battle on one famous occasion. In Egilsay, he spent the night before the meeting in prayer in the church, but he was then overcome by the followers of Earl Hakon before being sentenced to death. Magnus was only about 35 years old, but he showed no rancour, even comforting the man, Lifolf, a cook, detailed to do the deed. He was buried first in Earl Thorfinn's Minster of Christchurch at Birsay, but his grave soon became a place of pilgrimage and vision and the relics were transferred to Kirkwall.

As the seat of the earls of Orkney, Birsay had been a very important centre for both the Church and secular power, but now power was to shift to the east, to the small settlement of Kirkwall. There was already a small church here, dedicated to St Olaf Haraldson and situated down by the harbour, but in 1137 the great cathedral of St Magnus was founded and this provided an impetus for the rise in importance of the town. The project was originally the brainchild of Kol, the father of Earl Rognvald. Kol was a man of great vision who counselled his son to seek the divine assistance of St Magnus (who had been Rognvald's uncle), in his own struggle for power in the islands. In return, Rognvald was to vow to found a church in Kirkwall: 'more magnificent than any other in these islands'.*

*Hjaltalin and Goudie, *The Orkneyinga Saga, p. 99.*

No expense was spared in the construction of St Magnus Cathedral. The plans were ambitious: throughout Scotland only Dunfermline and Kelso had churches to rival the building that Kol envisaged. Masons who had worked at Durham and Dunfermline were hired, together with a whole range of craftsmen to work on the interior fittings. The population of the town must have spiralled in those early years. The masons and craftsmen worked fast, and by the 1150s the choir and transepts were ready for use, though completion of the whole building was to take over three centuries (in fact, work continued, on and off, into this century: some parts were not completely finished until 1976, and it could be argued that work on a cathedral never ends). The cathedral is the final resting place for the bones of St Magnus, and also those of Earl Rognvald, its founder, himself later elevated to the status of saint.

St Magnus Cathedral may be regarded as the high point of church building in Norse Orkney, and Christchurch Minster was undoubtedly important as well, but church building on a more

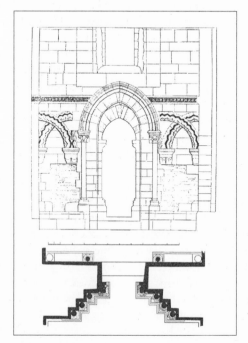

Figure 30.
St Magnus Cathedral, an architectual detail from the interior: the doorway in the south transept, drawn in the nineteenth century.

Figure 31.
St Magnus Cathedral,
the south aisle of
the nave in the
nineteenth century.

modest scale was going on all over the islands throughout the period. The map of Orkney is studded with evidence for small churches and chapels founded by the Norse: evidence for twenty-nine has been recorded on the island of Sanday alone. Many may have been for the private use of wealthy families, while others were for more general use. Their locations have been related to the administrative division of the land and it seems that they were organised from a central power, probably that of the earl. One particularly unusual church was built at Orphir in Mainland, by the same Earl Hakon Paulsson who had been responsible for the murder of Earl Magnus. After the murder he went on a pilgrimage to Rome and the Holy Land, and on his return home he built a church to St Nicholas next to his drinking hall. The design of this church was round, inspired by the Church of the Holy Sepulchre in Jerusalem, and its remains may be visited today. Elsewhere, some of these foundations survive simply as humps and bumps in grassy fields, while others have completely disappeared, but a remarkable number are reasonably well preserved (if sometimes as part of a later rebuilding), and may be visited, as at Tuquoy and Pierowall in Westray, St Mary's in Wyre, and St Magnus in the island of Egilsay.

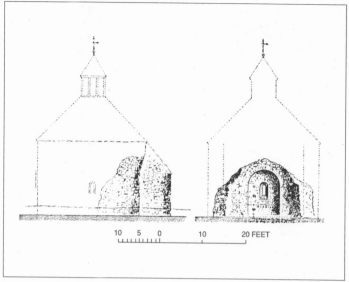

Figure 32. Elevations of the church at Orphir, drawn in the nineteenth century.

Castles

Norse Orkney saw considerable changes to the face of the islands. The grandeur of St Magnus Cathedral and the development of more substantial chapel sites mark a change in magnitude for local building traditions. There was a boom in architecture as developments in technology and style were imported and flourished locally, fuelled by both the availability of wealth to finance building work and the ambition to demand larger projects. The role of architecture to represent status was not lost on the local elite, many of whom built elaborate hall-houses around the islands. In this way, two-storey buildings became more common, emerging as a clear symbol of the way in which the power of the Church was entwined with that of the local aristocracy.

The wealthy Norse landowners not only built themselves chapels and fine drinking halls, a few also built simple fortified castles. The best known of these is Cubbie Roo's Castle on the small island of Wyre. Here oral tradition has preserved the name of the castle's builder to the present day, for the Orkneyinga Saga tells of a man named Kolbein Hruga, a wealthy landowner who farmed in Wyre and built a solid stone castle there. Only the lower courses of the castle's stonework survive today, but it is easy to see that it was a well-designed stronghold. The castle comprised double ditches and ramparts, one of stone, around a square tower that probably stood at least three storeys high. The tower walls are almost 2 metres thick and another saga describes how hard it was to attack. Kolbein Hruga seems to have designed his castle to serve as a refuge in times of trouble, as it is not big and the farm nearby is still known as the Bu of Wyre, which suggests that his main family home was here. Close to the farm and the castle stand the remains of St Mary's Church, a small chapel built in the late twelfth century, presumably for the same prosperous family.

Two other castle sites are mentioned in the Orkneyinga Saga, but both have long since disappeared and they cannot be identified with certainty. Other possible castle remains have been suggested by archaeologists, e.g. at the Wirk in Rousay, but so far nothing has been confirmed by excavation.

The Wealthy Heart of the Scandinavian World

Orkney was an important part of the Scandinavian world and it is clear that there were several wealthy families among the Norse inhabitants of Orkney. This is not surprising because not only are the islands a fertile place to farm, but also they lay at the heart of a great seafaring culture. Far from being the far-flung northern outpost that it is sometimes perceived as today, Orkney lay at the centre of a great network of water routes that connected Ireland to Scandinavia, and extended as far as Jerusalem and Constantinople, into Russia, and even to Greenland and North America. Many of the Norsemen were keen travellers at heart: they stayed at home to tend the farm business over the winter, and in the summer they ventured far afield in their ships.

No doubt, many of these seafaring Norsemen indulged in a spot of raiding: this is well recorded in the annals and sagas, and in this way they were able to bring home foreign goods to enhance their wealth. But commerce and economic expansion lay at the heart of Norse society, which also included many merchants and traders. Dublin was the main commercial centre at the time, and Orkney was geographically very well placed to benefit from the main economic routes between the western and southern countries and the Scandinavian homeland. Goods from many places were traded along these routes and some must have made their way to Orkney. The material goods from Norse-period excavations in Orkney include many items from overseas. In this way, considerable personal fortunes could be amassed, and there is evidence for this in items such as the fine brooch of precious metal and jewels from a woman's grave at Westness in Rousay. There are also hoards of fine objects of silver, such as those from Skaill and Burray. Although some archaeologists have interpreted these as traders' hoards rather than personal wealth, they still show the ready market for luxury goods that existed throughout the isles.

In Westray, James Barrett from Cambridge has been excavating the remains of a stone-built complex of buildings at Quoygrew to uncover evidence of a thriving settlement that was occupied from the ninth century AD into the 1930s. In the Norse period activity here focused on fish processing on an industrial scale, which left large middens of refuse. Locally caught cod and saithe were dried here before export to the growing urban centres of Europe, particularly around the Baltic. The evidence from Quoygrew reminds us of the scale at which local businesses could operate and the extent to which Orkney operated as part of the wider world.

Much of the wealth generated from these activities no doubt went to the Church, but some Orcadians also used it to extend their travels. The earls and their followers frequently journeyed to Norway, and south along the seaboards of England and Ireland. Some went further afield. Both Earl Hakon Paulsson and Earl Thorfinn made pilgrimages, and Earl Rognvald was away from the islands for two years on an expedition to the Holy Land that came to be known as a crusade. These men did not travel alone: the saga provides a wonderful description of Earl Rognvald's crusade and the adventures that he and his retinue got into, and Earl Hakon and Earl Thorfinn were also accompanied by their retainers. No doubt not everyone returned home, but the introduction of foreign experiences into the islands cannot have been without its influences.

At the same time, no doubt, there were foreign visitors to the islands, attracted by trading and other contacts abroad. Visitors would bring their own suite of goods and experiences.

Burial

The Norse inhabitants of Orkney certainly left enough, in both buildings and objects, to mark their lives in the islands. What about their burial practices? Not surprisingly, many Norse burials have been found throughout the islands, and these may broadly be divided into two: pre-Christian 'pagan' burials and Christian burials. The pre-Christian burials follow many different practices. There were cemeteries (two have been excavated: at Pierowall in Westray and at Westness in Rousay), and people were also buried in isolation (for example in the ruins of the Iron Age settlement at Gurness). Mounds were erected over some burials, while others were inserted into existing tumuli, and some were flat. Some burials were placed in stone-lined cists, others in earthen graves. Some people were buried without goods, though it was common for a few household belongings to be included, such as a knife and a sickle, or, for the women, sewing and weaving kits. A few graves (as at Westness in Rousay) included rich personal possessions. Many strata of society and belief were represented among the dead.

Many Norse pagan burials are quite spectacular: one of the best-known must be that excavated in 1992 during terrible winter storms at Scar in the island of Sanday where the remains were being washed into the sea. Here the outline of a boat could be distinguished from the pattern of iron rivets that had survived in the sand. Inside the boat, a burial chamber contained the remains of three bodies – a man, a woman and a child – as well as many personal belongings that showed them to have been wealthy. Alongside the man lay his arms, a sword in a wooden scabbard and arrows, together with more mundane objects such as a comb and a set of gaming pieces. The woman had a fine gilded brooch, as well as her household objects – spindle whorls and shears and a decorated whalebone plaque.

The Christian burials are quite different from these pagan remains: the new teaching was that bodies should be buried without goods, generally in simpler graves, and often close to a church or other religious site.

Christian Norse graves tend to be more difficult to recognise, because of the lack of datable objects, but a few have been identified. On rare occasions, later in the Norse period, a Christian burial was given a distinctive stone marker, known as a 'hogback' from its long humped shape. Hogback stones are in fact representations of buildings, with rows of carefully carved roof tiles that often stand out. There are four in Orkney today: two are on display in the Orkney Museum in Kirkwall (one came originally from the Cathedral of St Magnus); one may be visited at the twelfth-century chapel of St Boniface in Papa Westray; and the fourth is to be seen at Skaill in Deerness. The stone here has been moved into the Session House, though it was found in the churchyard, and excavations have uncovered the remains of a wealthy Norse farmstead nearby. The sagas tell us that in the eleventh century Skaill was the home of Thorkell Fostri, the right-hand man of Earl Thorfinn and an important character in Orcadian history.

Graffiti

There is one other Norse activity that has carried the atmosphere of these times down to the present day. They liked carving graffiti. The Norse Orcadians were surely not the first to indulge in this activity, and they have not been the last, but they have left a fine collection of runic messages carved on many of the ancient monuments that already littered the isles.

The best-known, and largest, collection of Norse graffiti was inscribed in Maeshowe sometime in the mid-twelfth century and they include the depiction of the famous 'Maeshowe Dragon'. Maeshowe was entered on more than one occasion: Earl Harald and some of his men sheltered from a snowstorm here; and later adventurers returning from travels with Earl Rognvald on his crusade broke into the tomb. The subjects of the messages include references to treasure. This was originally thought by archaeologists to be wishful thinking, because the Neolithic builders of Maeshowe would not have known precious metals, but recent excavation has suggested that Maeshowe may have been reused in the early Norse

```
1 ᚦᛅᛏ ᛁᚱ  ᚢᛁᚴᛁᚾᚴᛦ⋯⋯ᚴᛅᛦ ᛘᛁᚱ ᚼᛦ ᛏᛁᛚ    3 ᛒᚱᛅ ᚼᛟᚼ ᚦᛅᚾᛅ
  THAT IR UIKINKR⋯⋯ÆKOM UTIR HER TIL      BRÆ HOH THÆNA

2 ᚦᛅᛚᚠᚱ  ᚴᛟᛚᛒᛅᛁᚾᛋᛟᚾᚱ ᚱᛅᛁᛋᚱᛚᚾᛅᚱ ᚦᛁᛦ ᚼᛅᛘ
  HOLFR KOLBÆINSSONR RÆISRLNÆR THESÆR HAUT

4 ᚾᛁᛒᛗᛏᚱ ᚱᛅᛁᛋᛏ                5 ᚠᚢᚦᛟᚱᚴᚼᚾᛁᛅᛋᛏᛒᚢᚾᚢ
  UEMUNTR RÆIST                 FUTHORKHNIASTBYNU

6 ᛅᚱᚴᛅᛋᛟᚾᚱ  ᛋᛅᚼᚦᛁᛅ ᛅ ᚱᛟᛘᛘᛁ ᚦᛅᛁᛘ ᛁᚱ ᚼᛅᚾ ᚱᛁᛋᛏᚢ
  ORKASONR SAHTIE A RUNOM THÆIM IR HAN RISTU

7 ᚾᚢᛅᛁᚱᛁᚴᚢᛚᛏᚢᚱᛘᛁᚱᛁᚢᚴᚢᚱᛁᚱᚠᛅᛚᚼᚴ  ᚴᛁᛅᛒᛁᚴᛁᚢᛁᛚᛋᛅᚼᛁᛅᚾᛁᚱᛋᛟᛘᛅᛁᚱ
  NUAIRIKULTURMIRIUKURIRFALHK  KIÆBIKIUILSÆHIÆNIRSOMAIR

8 ᛁᚾᚴᛁᛒᛁᛟᚱᚼ ᚼᛁᚾ ᚠᛅᚼᚱᛅ ᛅᛚᚼᚴᛁᛅ ᛘᛟᚱᚼᚴ ᚴᛟᚾᛅ ᚼᛅᚠᛦ ᚠᛅᚱᛏ
  INGIBIORH HIN FAHRA ÆLHKIA MORHK KONA HÆFER FARET

  ᛚᚢᚦᛁᚾ ᚼᛦ ᛘᛁᚼᚴᛁᛚ ᛟᚠᛚᛅᛏᛁ        ᛅ ᚱ ᛚ ᛁ ᚴ ᚱ
  LUTHIN HER MIHKIL OFLATE         Æ R L I K R

9 ᚦᛟᚱᚾᛅ  ᛋᛅᚱᚦ ᚼᛅᛚᚼᛁ ᚱᛅᛁᛋᛏ          10 ᚦᛟᚱᛦ ᚠᛟᛘᛁᚱ
  THORNY SÆRTH HÆLHE RÆIST            THORER FOMIR

11 ᚱᛅᛁᛋᛏ ᚱᚢᚾᛅᚱ ᚦᛅᛋᚱ ᚠᚱᛅᛏᚱ ᛋᛁᚼᚢᚱᚦᛅᚱᛋᛟᚾᚱ
   RÆIST RUNAR THÆSÆR OFRAMR SIHURTHARSONR

12 ᛟᛏᛅᚱ ᚠᛁᛚᛅ ᚱᛅᛁᛋᛏ ᚱᚢᚾᛅᚱ ᚦᛁᛋᛅᚱ
   OTAR FILA RÆIST RUNAR THISAR
```

Figure 33. Some of the Norse runes carved inside Maeshowe. The runes have been much studied and they were clearly carved on several different occasions. One of the rune carvers has recently been identified as Thorhallr Asgrimsson, whose great-great-great-grandfather killed one Gaukr Trandillsson in Iceland. The story of Gaukr's death is told in *Njal's Saga* and 200 years later Thorhallr could not resist boasting in his runes of his prowess as a rune carver and of the antiquity and notoriety of his axe!

As with modern graffiti the content of the runic carvings can be somewhat doubtful, and some of those shown here have been translated as follows (from M. P. Barnes, 'The Interpretation of the Runic Inscriptions of Maeshowe', in Batey, C. E., Jesch, J. and Morris, C. D. (eds), *The Viking Age in Caithness, Orkney and the North Atlantic* (Edinburgh: Edinburgh University Press 1993):

2: E yjolfr Kolbeinssonr carved these runes high.

7: – it is told to me that treasure is hidden here extremely well. Few say as Oddr –

8: Ingibjorg the fair widow. Many a woman has gone bowed in here. A great show-off. Erlingr.

9: Þorny fucked. Helgi carved.

period, in which case it is possible that rich goods were buried here, either for safekeeping or as part of a later burial. As no goods have survived within the tomb, and the Norse graffiti writers were known to boast (in common with graffiti writers everywhere), the matter is still open to debate. The graffiti also tells of the ancestry and deeds of the Norsemen concerned, as well as citing the merits of various local ladies! Other Norse graffiti may be seen in the tomb at Unstan, as well as on one of the stones in the Ring of Brodgar.

NORSE SITES (see map, p. xxx)

1 St Magnus Cathedral, Kirkwall, Mainland   HY 449108

In the centre of town.

> 'The grandest and largest building in Orkney, dominating
> the town and a landmark from the sea.'*

Magnus was accepted as a saint in 1136, and work on the cathedral started in 1137, after his nephew Earl Rognvald won control of the earldom. The principal visionary behind the cathedral project seems to have been Kol, Rognvald's father (and Magnus' brother-in-law), who went on to supervise the building works. Kol brought in masons who had worked on the cathedrals of Durham and Dunfermline to the south. It was an ambitious undertaking, and the influence of the masons can be seen in the many similarities between this building and those of Dunfermline and Durham. Work began at the eastern end as was traditional for church building at the time, and within about fifteen years the choir was ready to be used as a scaled-down church, though the rest of the building would take another three centuries to complete. Not surprisingly, there are some architectural differences inside, due to the long building period (e.g. among the pillars of the nave which go from early twelfth century in design at the eastern end to late twelfth century further to the west), but the whole building is remarkably uniform in design. Red sandstone was quarried from near to Kirk-

*Gifford, *The Buildings of Scotland,* p. 311.

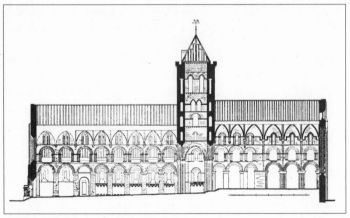

Figure 34. St Magnus Cathedral, section drawn in the nineteenth century.

wall for the cathedral, and mixed with yellow sandstone from Eday to give a very striking effect, both inside and out.

Inside the cathedral there are many interesting tombs and sculptures, both ancient and modern. Originally, it contained the graves of three famous Norse Orcadians: Bishop William, under whom work on the cathedral was started when the episcopal seat moved to Kirkwall; Earl Rognvald, who was canonised; and St Magnus, whose bones were moved here from Birsay. The remains of Bishop William were, however, removed in the nineteenth century, and the bones of the two saints are also no longer in their original resting places, though they do still lie in the cathedral. At first they may have been kept in public reliquaries on view in the choir, but at some stage the holy bones were placed for safekeeping in cavities in the pillars. During renovation work in the early twentieth century St Magnus' bones were discovered in a box (now on display in the Orkney Museum) in the south side pier, and the remains of St Rognvald lie in a similar cavity in a rectangular pier on the north side of the choir. The saints' bones have particularly personal touches: St Magnus' skull has been cleft with the axe blow from Lifolf the cook, about which we can read in the saga; and St Rognvald's skull also shows signs of the wounds which, according to the saga, led to his death while pursuing outlaws in Caithness.

The bones may have been moved as late as the Reformation, but it has also been suggested that access to relics such as these would have been controlled in earlier times to ensure their well-being. The exact date of the transferral to their hidden resting places therefore remains uncertain.

Work on a cathedral never finishes. The original building work may be said to have ended, but in the nineteenth century there was much restoration work, and this is still an ongoing process. As the sandstone is relatively soft and vulnerable to the elements, the decorated stonework and statues are particularly in need of monitoring and attention. There are also, still, changes made to the interior from time to time, though these are, of course, carefully controlled. In 1987 a new stained glass window for the west end of the nave was commissioned to celebrate the 850th anniversary of the cathedral. It is a good example of how modern additions may enhance a special place, even after considerable time, and this is, of course, quite in keeping with Orkney life, where earlier ceremonial centres such as the Brodgar Peninsula may well have been used and added to over the centuries.

In 1954 the Kirkwall Market Cross, dated to 1621, was moved from Broad Street into the cathedral for safekeeping.

Figure 35. View of St Magnus Cathedral in the nineteenth century.

2 Bishop's Palace, Kirkwall, Mainland HY 449108

Historic Scotland; signposted; in the centre of town.

The lowest floor of the Bishop's Palace dates back to Norse times, perhaps to the residency of Bishop William in the mid-twelfth century when the cathedral was being built and the seat of the episcopacy moved from Birsay to Kirkwall. At this time the palace was designed as a rectangular hall-house, with the main hall on the first floor, over a series of cellars that were used for storage and workshops. It would have been a grand building and incorporated the same decorative red and white bands of stonework as the cathedral across the street.

By the mid-sixteenth century the palace had fallen into disrepair, and at this time it was repaired and much altered by Bishop Robert Reid, so that little of the earlier building has survived beyond the lower courses of the walls. On the outer wall of the tower a statue of St Rognvald stands in a red sandstone niche: this is a modern replica and the original may be seen in Tankerness House Museum. The palace was further altered by Earl Patrick Stewart as part of the scheme in which he built the Earl's Palace close by.

In 1263, King Hakon Hakonson came here after his defeat at the Battle of Largs, and he died in the palace in that winter.

Figure 36. Kirkwall: the Bishop's Palace and St Magnus Cathedral in the nineteenth century.

3 St Olaf's Kirk, Kirkwall, Mainland   HY 450112

In St Olaf's Wynd.

Sometime after 1035, Earl Rognvald Brusison returned to Orkney and built a church by the harbour in Kirkwall dedicated to his foster-father, King Olaf Haraldson of Norway, who had been killed in battle five years earlier (and was later canonised). Earl Rognvald is noted as living in Kirkwall, and this is one of the earliest mentions of settlement here in the sagas. St Olaf's Kirk was the first church to be built in Kirkwall, and it is likely that the name of the town derives from this building. All that is left of the church today is a Romanesque archway of carved sandstone slabs, moved and rebuilt in St Olaf's Wynd. It is heavily weathered, but it gives an impression of the splendour of the original building. In the 1970s a hogback tombstone was found on the site of the original churchyard and moved to the Orkney Museum.

4 Brough of Birsay, Mainland   HY 239285

Historic Scotland; signposted; car park; causeway at low tide; care needed.

Before the Bishopric of Orkney moved to Kirkwall it was based at Birsay. The sagas relate that Earl Thorfinn built a minster, the Christchurch, here after his return from Rome in the mid-eleventh century, but it is likely that this, and the Bishop's Residence, were located in Mainland, beneath the modern village of Birsay. Nevertheless, the Norse remains in the Brough of Birsay are dominated by the ruins of a fine church and other buildings, and it is clear that there was an important community here as well.

At the centre of the present-day site here are the walls of the stone-built church, a small romanesque building which may have had a square tower at the west end. It still retains stone benches along the walls as well as various recesses and other details of the internal fitments. The present altar in the choir was built in 1934, and the ruins contain other fragments that indicate various alterations through the ages, such as the cross-wall which separates the choir from the apse and which is probably late medieval in date.

To one side of the church lies the graveyard, and to the north is a courtyard, enclosed by the remains of other buildings. This has added weight to the suggestion that there was an ecclesiastical community on the Brough of Birsay in Norse times, but there is little certain evidence for this. Nevertheless, all around lie the remains of ordinary Norse houses and there were once many more. Natural coastal erosion means that many structures have been washed into the sea, and this process still continues. For this reason, recent archaeological work has concentrated on examining the remains that are most at risk. From the results of this and earlier work have come details of both artefacts and structures that show that between the ninth and twelfth centuries a substantial and wealthy farming settlement flourished on this tidal island.

Between the church and the sea lies a complex of house remains that include foundations from several periods up to later medieval times, and among them fragments of a large hall and other structures have been identified. These incorporate such a level of sophistication, including the existence of heating and drainage systems and possible saunas, that it was originally suggested that they might be the site of the halls of Earl Sigurd and his son Earl Thorfinn. It is now thought more likely that the settlement of the earls themselves lay on the Mainland of Orkney near to the modern village

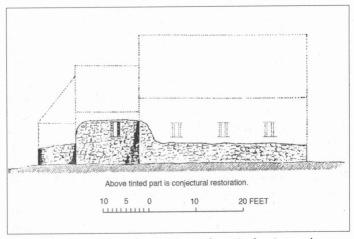

Above tinted part is conjectural restoration.

10 5 0 . 10 20 FEET

Figure 37. Elevation of the chapel in Birsay, drawn in the nineteenth century.

of Birsay, but the ruins on the Brough of Birsay indicate that there was a wealthy Norse household here as well.

Above the church lie the remains of a variety of humbler Norse structures. These include small single-roomed foundations as well as simple longhouses in a traditional style, with bowed walls and stone benches inside. The Norse community on the Brough of Birsay was clearly numerous and diverse.

The church itself was built late in the Norse period, in the twelfth century, but there is evidence that it lay over an earlier, Early Christian, chapel dating back to Pictish times. So far, no trace has been found of any religious foundation in the earlier Norse period and it has been suggested that the community was purely secular at this time.

5 Maeshowe, Mainland   HY 318127

Historic Scotland; signposted; car park.

The Neolithic tomb of Maeshowe was entered by Norsemen on more than one occasion. It may even have been used for the burial of a wealthy chieftain in the ninth century, though the evidence for this is still scanty: the bank around the monuments was rebuilt at that time, and later graffiti carvers speak of a great treasure that once lay in the tomb.

More certainly, Maeshowe contains one of the largest collections of runic graffiti in existence, which relates to more than one visit by Orcadian Norsemen in the twelfth century. The messages tell of different things, from spectacular events such as the great storm that drove a group of warriors to seek shelter inside the tomb (on which occasion two of the men went mad) and the removal of the treasure, to more mundane matters such as the beauty of a particular local woman and the skilled rune-making talents of one particular rune carver. As might be expected from graffiti today, interpretations of the messages vary: some have suggested that the Norsemen were making idle or cynical boasts, while others take them very seriously and they have been used to help with dating particular events. At a mundane, but remarkable, level they suggest that literacy was commonplace through Norse society in a way that would not be achieved again for many centuries.

6 Brough of Deerness

HY 596087

OIC; signposted; car park; steep, rocky footpath best accessible at low tide; care needed.

The remains of a rectangular stone chapel in a walled enclosure lie amidst the grass-covered foundations of a settlement of Norse houses on the top of this high, steep-sided promontory. At the landward side of the promontory there is a rampart which would enhance the natural defences of the site.

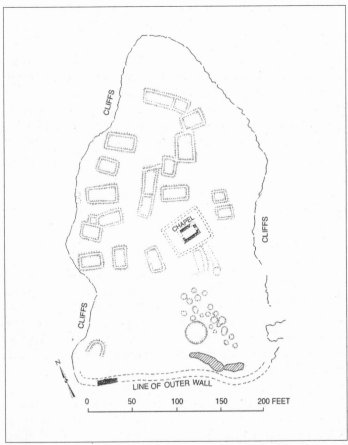

Figure 38. Plan of the chapel and buildings on the Brough of Deerness.

Recent excavation has confirmed the Norse date of the chapel, and showed that it replaced an earlier timber building that was founded in the tenth century. The Brough of Deerness was well-known as a place of pilgrimage in later times and it was once suggested that the remains may be those of a religious community, but the recent excavation indicates that it was purely a secular, defended settlement. Clustered around the chapel lie the remains of over thirty dwellings and outbuildings and the evidence suggests that this was the home of a wealthy chieftain and his retainers. This is not only indicated by the prominent location of the site but also by the finds, which include many high-status objects such as gaming pieces and a board, finely decorated bone combs and evidence of metalworking.

The flat top of the promontory is covered with broad, shallow pits: these are the result of its having been used for target practice from the sea during the Second World War. The visibility of the upstanding remains made them a convenient target, but the observant will note that the pits show a consistent error, always landing to one side of the ruins; whether this was a deliberate attempt to preserve the ruins, or merely the result of fortuitous accident, is not certain.

7 Skaill Hogback Tombstone, Deerness, Mainland

HY 588063

Inside the Session House of the modern church.

The present church at Skaill was built at the end of the eighteenth century, but an earlier church with twin round towers was recorded by the Reverend Low in 1774 and it is likely that the site is at least Norse in age. This fine tombstone was found in a corner of the graveyard and must date to the earlier church. It is a typical hogback and has a depiction of four rows of roof tiles carved along its length. It is made of red sandstone and dates to the late eleventh or early twelfth century.

Skaill is recorded in the Orkneyinga Saga as the home of Thorkell Fostri, foster-father to Earl Thorfinn, and excavations to the north of the church have uncovered traces of a high-status Norse settlement, here as well as earlier Pictish remains.

Figure 39. The church at Skaill in Deerness, drawn by Low in 1774.

8 St Nicholas Church and other remains, HY 334044
   Orphir, Mainland

Historic Scotland & OIC; signposted; display and car park.

This is the only medieval circular church to survive in Scotland, albeit in a fragmentary fashion. It was founded about 1120 by Earl Hakon Paulsson (responsible for the murder of St Magnus), who had been on a pilgrimage to Jerusalem and must have seen the circular Church of the Holy Sepulchre there. Round churches of this type were briefly popular at the time. Only the apse survives intact at Orphir, but the plan of the nave has been revealed and there are early accounts of its appearance.

Earl Hakon lived at Orphir, and the Orkneyinga Saga describes the buildings here in vivid detail:

'There was a great drinking-hall at Orphir, with a door in the

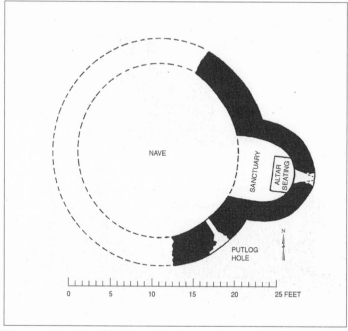

NAVE

SANCTUARY

ALTAR
SEATING

PUTLOG
HOLE

N

0 5 10 15 20 25 FEET

Figure 40. Remains of the Norse church at Orphir.

south wall near the eastern gable, and in front of the hall, just a few paces down from it, stood a fine church. On the left as you came into the hall was a large stone slab, with a lot of big ale vats behind it, and opposite the door was the living room.'*

Recent excavations have uncovered the remains of a large building just outside the modern churchyard enclosure, and this may well be the remains of the 'great drinking-hall', though more work is necessary to confirm this. Nearby lie modern farm buildings, and close to them traces of a horizontal watermill have been uncovered. This mill also goes back to Norse times, and it is the earliest evidence for this type of mill in Orkney. The Bu of Orphir has clearly always been a fertile and important place for settlement.

*Hjaltalin and Goudie, *The Orkneyinga Saga.*

9 Boat-house, Moaness, Rousay

HY 377293

Private; on Rousay Heritage Walk.

The 'noust', or boat-house, on the south side of the headland was excavated in the late 1970s by a team from Norway, who came to excavate an important Norse cemetery here. There is little to see today. Nousts were shelters into which individual ships and boats could be pulled for shelter during storms and at times when they were not needed, such as in the height of winter. Nousts were generally dug into the sloping shore, and their protection might be enhanced by building low stone walls around the cut.

The excavations here also uncovered the site of a Norse farmsteading, as well as the cemetery, which included the grave of a wealthy young woman who had been laid to rest with three richly decorated brooches. This complex seems to date from the earlier years of the Norse settlement in Orkney.

10 St Mary's Church, Westness, Rousay

HY 373301

On Rousay Heritage Walk.

This church was founded in the twelfth century. It is now very ruinous, and most of the stonework dates to later building activities. In the nineteenth century the gables were shored up with thick buttresses, but they are still very unstable.

11 The Wirk, Rousay

HY 373302

On Rousay Heritage Walk.

Just outside the churchyard of St Mary's lie the grassed-over remains of a stone tower, from which the foundations of a large hall-like building project. This has been compared with the remains of Cubbie Roo's Castle in Wyre, and it may represent the remains of a substantial, fortified Norse building, but more recent sixteenth-century origins have also been suggested. Only excavation could help to clear up the mystery.

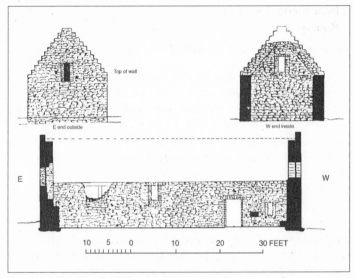

Figure 41. The chapel at Westness in Rousay in the nineteenth century.

12 Eynhallow Church; Eynhallow   HY 359288

Historic Scotland; information on access to Eynhallow available from Visit Orkney.

In 1851 the small settlement on the island of Eynhallow was evacuated due to a fever epidemic and the roofs were removed from the island dwellings in order to stop the inhabitants from reoccupying them. As a result of this it was discovered that one range of houses had been adapted from a well-preserved Romanesque church, built in the twelfth century. The sagas suggest that there was a monastic settlement here at this time, and the other buildings beside the church may well represent its remains, though as they too have since been used as dwellings, it is difficult to substantiate this.

Though the original structure has clearly suffered from its adaptation to use as dwellings, it is possible to get an impression of the grandeur of the monastic buildings here. The church had a rectangular nave and chancel, divided by an arch, and at the west end there is a solid porch that some architectural historians have suggested may have formed the base of a stone tower. Many of the

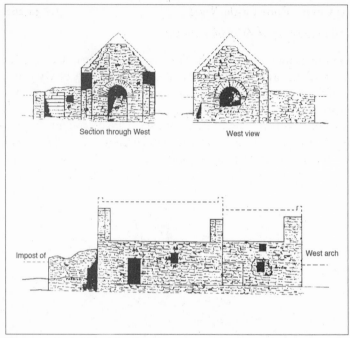

Figure 42. Eynhallow Church in the nineteenth century.

internal fittings, such as the aumbries and cupboard in the nave, probably date from the time when the building was used for housing, but it is still possible to make out various original features, such as the narrow doorway to the west, above which three slabs have been set in a triangular formation.

It has been suggested that there may have been an even earlier Celtic monastery in Eynhallow. Its name means 'Holy Isle' in Old Norse, which suggests that its religious association was already in place when the Norse arrived, and popular mythology endows the island with particular supernatural qualities: it was said to disappear and reappear from time to time. (This quality need not alarm modern visitors: it has since been laid to rest with a ritual journey to the island in which an iron knife was sunk into the turf to bind it.)

These ruins were consolidated in 1897 by the architect Lethaby.

13 Cubbie Roo's Castle, Wyre   HY 441262

Historic Scotland; footpath from jetty.

Shortly before 1150, a wealthy farmer named Kolbein Hruga built a fine stone castle on a low hill to the north-west side of Wyre. His building was mentioned in two separate sagas: the Orkneyinga Saga; and later the Hakonar Saga, which describes how hard it was to attack in 1231. The castle comprised a small, roughly square, stone tower set inside two rock-cut ditches with a stone wall between them and a rampart on the outer side. It is likely that the tower was at least three storeys high, and the walls are about 2

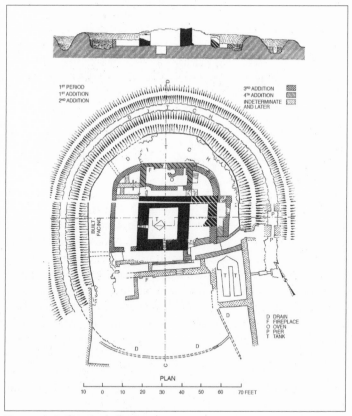

Figure 43. Cubbie Roo's Castle.

metres thick. The entrance was on the first floor, and wooden ladders provided internal access between the floors. It is not large and would probably only have been inhabited in times of trouble. The modern farm close by is called 'The Bu', and may have been where Kolbein Hruga had his drinking-hall and farmstead. There is also a twelfth-century church here (below).

In later times, when defence was no longer necessary, the southern line of defences was demolished to make way for less substantial buildings.

14 St Mary's Chapel, Wyre   HY 443262

Historic Scotland.

This rectangular chapel, close to the site of Cubbie Roo's Castle, was built in the twelfth century, probably by Kolbein Hruga (Cubbie Roo), or his son Bjarni, who became the third bishop of St Magnus Cathedral in Kirkwall. The chapel was restored in the nineteenth century, and during the excavation work a grave was found which contained the remains of a large man: local speculation has suggested that this was Kolbein Hruga himself.

15 St Magnus Church, Egilsay   HY 466303

Historic Scotland; footpath from pier.

This church was built about 1136 to mark the martyrdom of Saint Magnus *c.* 1116. It replaced an earlier church nearby, in which the saga tells that Earl Magnus prayed before his death. Churches with round towers like this are known to have been fashionable at the time, in both Orkney and Norway, but this is the only surviving example in Orkney. The tower was originally higher than it is today, possibly reaching almost 20 metres, and it is recorded as having a conical stone roof. The tower was defensive as well as religious in nature – it could only be entered from inside the church – and there was a curious arrangement of windows: the ground floor window faces south; the first floor faces west; the second floor, east; and the third floor has four windows, one to each main point of the compass. The nave and chancel were rectangular and included a second storey to the chancel for the priest's lodgings. St Magnus

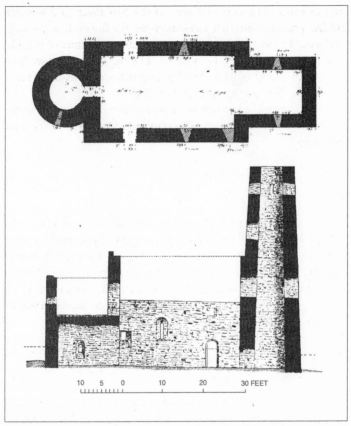

Figure 44. Nineteenth-century drawings of the church in Egilsay.

church was in use up to the early nineteenth century, which is when the tower was lowered, owing to the fragile condition of the upper levels.

16 Quoygrew, Westray   HY 443507

Local restoration of the site.

The site at Quoygrew was discovered in the 1970s due to the erosion of midden on the shore; it was excavated in the early twenty-first century and the remains were consolidated as a local heritage site.

Figure 45. A view of the church in Egilsay in the nineteenth century.

The first settlement here took place in the tenth century and comprised a small Norse farmstead built of turf. By the twelth century, however, there was a substantial stone hall, the occupants of which were able to accumulate substantial wealth through the processing and export of fish. Cod and saithe were caught and dried for export to the emerging urban centres of the Baltic and further south. Not surprisingly this activity led to the build-up of large piles of fish bones. Later on the focus of the site returned to farming: the remains of a medieval farmstead were found to overlie the Norse hall and the ruins of a nineteenth-century farm may still be seen just inland of the preserved site. This was abandoned in the 1930s.

17 The Lady Kirk, Pierowall, Westray   HY 439488

Historic Scotland.

Pierowall was an important settlement in Norse times, with a sheltered harbour and a large Norse cemetery, remains of which have been found in the dunes close to the present village. Grave goods from the burials suggest that this was an active trading centre. The ruins of the church on the sea front are largely seventeenth-century, but they incorporate traces of an earlier thirteenth-century Norse building.

18 Cross Kirk, Tuquoy, Westray   HY 455431
Historic Scotland.

This chapel was built in the twelfth century, but later extended. To the west lie substantial ruins that date from the same period. Recent excavations of these remains suggest that there was an important late Norse settlement here and the saga relates that one Hafliki Thorkelsson lived in the area.

19 St Boniface Church and Hogback Tomb,   HY 488527
    Papa Westray
OIC.

St Boniface Church has its origins in the twelfth century, though it has been much altered and extended, especially by the construction of a private burial-enclosure in the chancel. In the graveyard lies a fine twelfth-century hogback tombstone made of red sandstone and with three rows of roof tiles depicted on either side. St Boniface is likely to be an old foundation: it has been suggested as the seat of the Pictish bishopric of Orkney and two Early Christian cross slabs were discovered here earlier this century, one may now be seen in Tankerness House Museum in Kirkwall, and the other is with the National Museums of Scotland in Edinburgh. The Church of St Boniface was in use into the 1920s, and recent excavations have revealed both Iron Age and Pictish settlement in the vicinity. Traces of a large roundhouse, inhabited in the sixth century BC, were also uncovered.

Transfer to Scotland:
Scottish Earls in Orkney

The Decline of Norse Power

Although Orkney continued as an essentially Norse earldom, from the late twelfth century it was to come under increasing political influence from Scotland. The earls of Orkney, while Norse, were also members of the Scottish aristocracy and related to other Scottish nobles by both birth and marriage. They often held lands in Scottish territory, such as Caithness, and they travelled widely, making journeys across the North Sea to the Norwegian court in Bergen as well as to the Scottish court on the mainland to the south. In order to maintain their own power they had to tread a fine line to balance their allegiance between both the Scottish and Norwegian courts.

It has been argued that the political activities of Harald Maddadsson led to the Scottish Crown coming north to consolidate its power in Sutherland and Caithness and thus to its increasing force in Orkney. He was succeeded by his two sons, John and David, who ruled jointly, but the earldom was still in rebellion against the political powers of both Scotland and Norway. Although allegiance to the Norwegian Crown was maintained, the earls were deeply involved in Scottish affairs. Earl David died in 1214, and Earl John continued to tread a wary path, trying to placate both of his powerful neighbours. He made several visits to the Norwegian court, and was forced to conclude various treaties with Scotland, as a result of one of which his daughter became a hostage at the Scottish court. Earl John also faced internal competition for power within Orkney, and as a consequence of this he was murdered in 1231 in a drunken brawl in a pub cellar in Thurso. His death seems somehow ignominious as a finale to the great traditions in fighting and statesmanship of his predecessors, but it marked the end of the line. In a sad twist of fate, many of his family were drowned when their ship went down as they were returning to Orkney the following year, and so the earldom passed from his direct line to that of his Scottish kinsmen, the earls of Angus, though their allegiance stayed rooted with the royal house of Norway.

In contrast to their predecessors, at first the Angus earls seem to have lived more peacefully and meddled less in the rougher side of international affairs. During their time, there was increasing contact with, and involvement in, the Scottish court, but Orkney remained essentially Norse in character. The bishopric, for example, remained attached to Trondheim. In 1263, however, the problems of the balance of power came to the fore once more as relations between Scotland and Norway deteriorated. In that year a massed Norwegian fleet under King Hakon made an expedition to the west with the aim of reviving and consolidating Norwegian power. They attempted to land at Largs, on the Ayrshire coast, but were repelled by the Scots. This action was later to be known as the Battle of Largs and after it Norse influence elsewhere in Scotland was to wane. Although Orkneymen had been involved in the expedition, the impact in Orkney was not great, though Hakon himself died in Orkney in the winter following the battle, before he could return home. In the face of poor weather and declining health he had drawn up his ships at Houton, rather than attempt the stormy North Sea crossing, and he settled into the Bishop's Palace in Kirkwall, where he was to pass his last few weeks, listening to stories of the lives of the saints and the sagas of his ancestors. His body was laid to rest in St Magnus Cathedral, before being transferred to Bergen in 1264.

The Maid of Norway

In 1286 another event occurred which was to entwine even deeper the relations between Orkney, Norway and Scotland, and this event has remained enshrined in popular memory. This was the untimely death of Alexander III of Scotland, leaving as his sole heir a three-year-old granddaughter, Margaret, daughter of King Eric of Norway. Margaret's mother, Alexander's daughter, had died in childbirth, and following Alexander's death four years of intense diplomatic scheming ensued, in which it was arranged that the little princess, who was known as the Maid of Norway, should come into her kingdom, travelling via her father's territories in the north. She was to come to Scotland through Orkney, but matters did not end there: the English crown was also involved (through Edward I), and it had been arranged that she should marry Edward, the English Prince of Wales (later to become Edward II).

Margaret's marriage was clearly intended to strengthen the diplomatic union between England and Scotland, but things were not to be as the diplomats intended. Much myth surrounds the ending of the story: the facts are that the royal party set out by sea in September 1290, with the Bishop of Bergen to accompany the seven-year-old princess. By the time they approached the Orkney shores things had gone horribly wrong and Margaret died, either at sea or when she got to Orkney. Severe seasickness brought on by savage autumn storms is reputed to have been the cause. Though she had been Queen of Scotland, Margaret never completed her journey: her body was taken back to Bergen to be buried, and her grave may be visited there today.

The Sinclairs

After the death of the Maid of Norway the earls of Orkney were content to settle on the periphery of troubled events elsewhere. Scotland plunged first into the Wars of Independence and then into a series of wars with England, while Norway had both internal and external problems. These events impinged on Orkney, but matters were not as deeply entwined as they had been before. In the 1320s, the line of the Angus earls died out, and, after some dispute, in 1379 the islands came into the hands of another Scottish family, this time represented by Henry Sinclair of Roslin near Edinburgh. In Orkney Henry's political allegiance was still to the Norwegian crown, though his connections with the Scottish court were stronger than those of previous earls. He was keen on the development of his northern dominions; he spent much time there and was responsible (in defiance of the King of Norway) for the building of a strong castle in Kirkwall in front of the cathedral (sadly nothing survives of this building today).

Henry Sinclair is also reputed to have been something of an

adventurer. There is a story that he had in his service two Venetians, Nicolo and Antonio Zeno, who left an account of their time in the north. There is much exaggeration and fable in this account, but some would see a thread of truth in the tale. Among other things, it implies that Henry, together with the Zenos, made an expedition to Greenland, where they met with the Inuit tribes.

The years that followed were full of petty fighting: there were still challenges to Sinclair power in the islands, and at the same time long-standing differences with Hebrideans and other neighbours came to the fore. Nevertheless, the life of common folk changed little: they were still primarily farmers with livestock and crops to look after, they lived in long stone houses, worshipped in the local church, and owed allegiance to the powerful landlords. Though the current houses are modern, many Orkney farm sites show a great continuity of settlement from Norse times. This is particularly so in islands such as Sanday, where many farms sit high on raised mounds that cover the buried settlement remains of former times. The sea was still important, and some Orcadians would follow their lord away from the isles to fight, but the raiding also took place at home: English attacks on Orkney and Orcadian fishermen are recorded from early in the 1400s, and it was in one of these attacks that Earl Henry died in about 1400.

Transfer to Scotland

Politically, the Sinclairs maintained control after Henry's death. They kept up necessary allegiance to Scandinavia, though they were really a Scots dynasty and the islands' links with Scotland were becoming ever closer. Then, in 1468, everything was to change. In this year, a marriage agreement was effected between another Margaret, daughter of King Christian I of Norway and Denmark, and James III of Scotland. The Danish king wished to provide a royal dowry for his daughter, but he was short of cash and pledged Orkney to Scotland in lieu of paying out the sum of 50,000 florins of the Rhine. It seems that he, and later kings, fully intended to settle the debt and reclaim Orkney, but the sum was never made up, and Shetland was soon included in the bargain, to cover the final 10,000 florins that he could not find.

With this transaction Orkney ceased to be a politically Scandinavian earldom, and became a Scottish earldom. The close ties that had been forged with the Scottish neighbours now became stronger and penetrated all levels of society from the aristocracy to the local farmers and townsfolk. An increasing Scots influx to the islands helped spread this influence, and the Church was also responsible for strengthening Scottish links. These changes were not, of course, instantaneous: Norn, the old Norse language, was still spoken in rural areas of Orkney up to the late eighteenth century, but Scottish laws and customs came gradually to replace Norse ways and taxes and eventually the bishopric of Orkney passed from Trondheim to St Andrews in Fife.

It was at this time that the Scottish custom of using surnames became commonplace. Though some surnames are known from earlier times, the Norse families had generally maintained the traditional patronymic system of naming children after their father. It has been argued that the allocation of new names to families is responsible for the large number of placenames to be found among Orkney surnames. In the search for a suitable designation, many people were named after their parish or farm: Rendall; Isbister; Mainland.

At first, the Scottish Sinclairs maintained their power and bought up more land in the islands, but they were not without their own problems as different factions within the family competed for control. This resulted, in 1529, in the Battle of Summerdale between two Sinclair cousins. The battle took place on the moorlands to the south of Stenness and involved an army of Orcadians, led by the cadet branch of the family, routing an invading army, mainly of Caithnessmen led by the Earl of Caithness, who was of the senior branch. The victory of the cadet side did not, however, end the problems of the Sinclairs. In 1540 the Scottish King James V himself was prompted by worries over events in Orkney to visit the islands as part of a royal progress round Scotland. By the late sixteenth century a new family, the Stewarts, was in power.

The Stewart Earls

Sixteenth-century Orkney was seen as a place of opportunity, and several new aristocratic families, such as the Bothwells and the Balfours, came to make their mark in Orkney, often initially on church business in which both the royal family and Scottish nobles were intimately involved. These entrepreneurs were generally interested in making money, and there was much intermarriage. Not surprisingly this led to much internal feuding and, in the mid-1560s, power in the islands was granted by Mary, Queen of Scots, to her half-brother Robert Stewart, illegitimate son of James V. The Stewart earls, Robert and his son, Patrick, are remembered even today for the hardship and cruelty of their times, and this period was to herald an all-time low for the people of Orkney. Though it is frequently pointed out that others, both before and after them, had also oppressed the islanders, the memory of the Stewart earls is particularly bitter.

Under the Stewarts, life for the ordinary farmers and merchants of Orkney was subject to a series of restrictions and hurdles. Lands were frequently appropriated, rents and taxes were raised, and trade could only take place under Stewart licence. All ferry traffic was under strict control and forced labour was introduced. As people struggled to survive, the farmlands became impoverished and even the Orkney landowners often found themselves in dispute with the earls, especially Earl Patrick. At the same time, however, some landed gentry flourished, and several elegant houses were built throughout the islands.

The Stewarts were men with a vision, keen to demonstrate the semi-royal status of their family through their lifestyle and palaces. They drew upon fashionable ideals from Renaissance Europe and in this way they were responsible for introducing new ideas into the islands. For the first time Orkney did not look solely to its old Scandinavian roots for cultural inspiration; the Stewarts brought ideas from further south and east. In the long run the Stewart finances and political connections were not able to support their grandiose ideals, but even so, they left a lasting mark on the islands.

In 1569 Earl Robert started work on a fine palace at Birsay. This was an elegant building set around a courtyard and well-appointed with gardens and greens on the outside. It contrasted greatly with Gilbert Balfour's castle, built in the 1560s at Noltland in the island of Westray, which had been a strong, defensive structure, with an unusually high number of gun loops all around the walls. The palace at Birsay had stylish glazed windows, which gave onto both the inner courtyard and the outside of the building; it was designed to make a clear statement about the new earls of Orkney. At the same time, many local landowners followed suit and less ostentatious dwellings began to spring up on smaller estates. Times were undoubtedly still troubled, but the more prosperous lairds could begin to think more of comfort, and houses such as Langskaill in the island of Gairsay and Carrick House in Eday show the combination of defence and elegance that had quickly become the norm.

The development of Kirkwall, too, reflects the dichotomy between defence and comfort. The merchants were generally prosperous, there was still wealth coming in from the land and they wished to make use of it, but there were also uncertainties. From the early 1400s there had been problems with English and other raids on the islands, slaving and harrying the fishermen, and in August 1557 the English fleet landed at Kirkwall. The town was bombarded and partly burnt, but two days later they were driven out by the local defence. Although in this case it was a distinct

Figure 46. A nineteenth-century view of the Earl's Palace at Birsay with the church in the background.

Figure 47. The exterior of Noltland Castle in the nineteenth century, showing the numerous gun loops.

defeat of the English and the admiral, Sir John Clere, was drowned trying to swim back to his ship, this was a clear sign of continuing problems. Nevertheless, local merchants were confident enough to expand and look forward, and a number of fine buildings in Kirkwall date from this time.

By 1574 the bishopric of Orkney was using a fine town house in Kirkwall, Tankerness House. This incorporated earlier buildings and served as a deanery building for the cathedral, having been converted to a family home by Gilbert Fulzie, Kirkwall's first Protestant priest. Over the road, to the side of the cathedral, Earl Patrick Stewart started work on an elaborate palace (the Earl's Palace) in 1607. This was an ambitious building, which drew on novel Renaissance influences, and as part of it Earl Patrick was also responsible for an extension and alterations to the neighbouring Bishop's Palace, an old building founded under the Norse earls in the twelfth century. Despite his wealth, however, Earl Patrick overstretched himself. He went bankrupt and his political scheming led to his

Figure 48. Tankerness House, Kirkwall, in the nineteenth century.

imprisonment (originally for debt) in Dumbarton in 1610.

Things did not go well for the Stewarts. Earl Patrick despatched his son, Robert, to collect rents and debts in Orkney and he made two ill-fated trips north. Robert Stewart went about his tasks with heavy-handed zeal and his occupation of Kirkwall Castle and other prominent buildings during the second of these trips was quickly seen as a rebellion against King James. This resulted in the raising of a government army to be sent to the isles with cannon from Edinburgh Castle to restore Crown control. In the end, both Earl Patrick and his son were executed within a few weeks of each other in Edinburgh in 1615. The reign of the Stewarts was ended and Orkney passed to the Earls of Morton.

The Seventeenth Century

In 1611 Norse Law was finally abolished, and local administration was managed by a series of tacksmen appointed by the earls. There was a general climatic deterioration, and this, coupled with the previous impoverishment, meant that rents and taxes became harsher and harsher. Many farmers had to give up, and poverty was rife. Famines became common, and even some landowners went bankrupt. Life for the average Orcadian was to take a while to improve, and the seventeenth century was one of poverty and agricultural exhaustion for most people.

In the mid-seventeenth century Kirkwall was occupied by a Cromwellian garrison from the south. The Cathedral of St Magnus was used for the stabling of horses, but there was little other mark on the Orcadians beyond the introduction of one or two innovations (such as, legend has it, locks and keys). Things were so bad that one of Cromwell's soldiers left a poor description of his hosts in 1652: 'Their schooles of learning are in every house, and their first lesson is to hunt the louse.'*

By 1750, however, life was improving: various agricultural improvement schemes were underway; communications were opening up; and local industry was increasing. The Orcadians at this time were described by Mackenzie as: 'kind without caressing, civil without ceremony, and respectful without compliment'.**

By this time, the earldom of Orkney was no longer politically connected to the islands, and Orkney had once more entered a new phase.

THE SCOTTISH EARLS SITES (see map, p. xxx)

1 Bishop's Palace, Kirkwall, Mainland   HY 449108

Historic Scotland; signposted; in the centre of town.

In the mid-sixteenth century Bishop Robert Reid rebuilt and enlarged the original Norse Palace, which had fallen into disrepair. He maintained the ground floor storerooms and the first floor hall, but he added two well-lit floors above the hall, as well as a five-storey round tower on the north-west corner. This tower contained

*Emerson, J. (attributed), *Poetical description of Orkney* (1652).
**Mackenzie, M., *Survey of the Orkney and Lewis Islands* (1750).

Figure 49. The Bishop's Palace at Kirkwall, from the Rev. Barry's *History*, published in 1805.

his private apartments and it rose high above the town, with a square cap-house and covered parapet. On the outer wall of the tower a weathered statue stands in a red sandstone niche: this is a likeness of Saint Rognvald (now a modern copy).

This must have been an imposing building in the centre of Kirkwall, but it is hard to know exactly what it looked like because it was also added to and altered in about 1600 by Earl Patrick Stewart as part of the work on the palace that he was building for himself close by.

2 Earl's Palace, Kirkwall, Mainland HY 449107

Historic Scotland; signposted; in the centre of town.

Work on this palace began in the early seventeenth century for Earl Patrick Stewart. Architects agree that it must have been a magnificent building in its heyday, drawing upon new influences, though Earl Patrick was one of Orkney's most hated landowners and the palace was largely built with forced labour. It is an L-plan in shape, and maintains the traditional arrangement of giving the ground floor over to vaulted storerooms, a kitchen, and workrooms, with the main apartments on the first floor. There was originally one more floor, but little trace of this survives.

The original entrance would have been very imposing: it was ornately decorated with three tiers of heraldic panels above the door, which was flanked by ribbed columns. A broad staircase rose to the first floor, where the great hall is situated. To either side of the entrance to the hall are small vaulted rooms, one was used by guests waiting to see the earl and the other by the earl's major-domo. The hall itself was over 16 metres long, and included two fireplaces and fine, high oriel windows. It is recorded that there was painted decoration in several rooms inside the palace, and it seems likely that the great hall was one of them.

Despite its elegance, the Earl's Palace had a short life. It was completed about 1607, and passed quickly through a series of hands, including various Orkney bishops and the Earl of Morton and his son. By 1705, however, it is recorded that it had fallen into disrepair and was not fit for habitation. By the mid-eighteenth century the roof had been stripped off so that the materials could be made use

Figure 50. The Earl's Palace, Kirkwall, in the nineteenth century.

Figure 51.
The Earl's Palace, Kirkwall,
a detail of the main entrance,
drawn in the nineteenth
century.

of in other local buildings. Nevertheless, the Earl's Palace has always been an important building at the centre of Kirkwall, and in the 1870s there was a proposal to restore and reroof it by the architect David Bryce, who had been contracted to design a new Sheriff Court. While this might have restored some of its former glory, it would have been a drastic alteration to the building, and so the modern visitor may be thankful that it was not undertaken. Today the palace ruins survive as a mute testament to the wealth, dominance, elegance and ambition of the seventeenth-century aristocracy.

3 Tankerness House (The Orkney Museum), HY 448108
Kirkwall, Mainland

OIC; signposted; now a museum in the centre of town.

Tankerness House was the archdeaconry for St Magnus Cathedral. Over the entrance gateway there is an armorial panel which bears the date 1574 and the initials of Master Gilbert Fulzie, one of the archdeacons who lived here and was responsible for the conversion of a range of pre-existing ecclesiastical buildings into a private home.

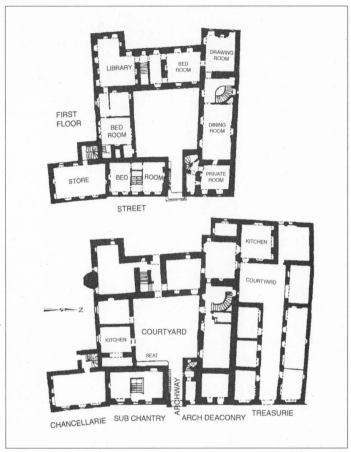

Figure 52. Nineteenth-century plans of Tankerness House, Kirkwall.

The north wing, which lies gable-on to the street, dates to the sixteenth century and is the oldest part of the house, which was enlarged and remodelled in the eighteenth century when it passed to the Baikies, wealthy merchants who also had a country estate in Tankerness (hence the name). The garden is also open to the public and includes the Groatie Hoose, a folly built from the ballast of the Brig *Revenge* which had been captained by John Gow, a notorious (and shortlived) local pirate.

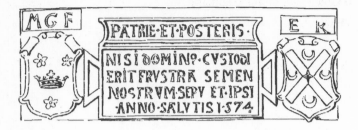

Figure 53. Tankerness House, Kirkwall: detail of the inscription over the main entrance drawn in the nineteenth century.

4 The Girnel, Kirkwall, Mainland

HY 448113

Private; on Harbour Street.

This store was built in the seventeenth century to hold grain paid in rents to the earl. Grain was an important export from the islands in return for goods that were locally scarce such as timber. To one side of the store stands the Girnel Keeper's House, which was built in 1643.

5 Hall of Tankerness, Tankerness, Mainland

HY 524088

Private.

Like many Orkney houses, the Hall as it stands today incorporates building work from many periods. It was started in the mid-sixteenth century for William Groat, who had recently bought the estate of Tankerness. There were many additions and changes to the house, including the erection of an iron pavilion encircled by a veranda in the nineteenth century, when a conservatory was also built. The buildings include a screen wall and low circular tower, as well as various sheds and offices, and a steading with a smithy.

In the 1630s the estate passed to the Baikie family, who also acquired a town residence in Kirkwall at about the same time. They named their town house Tankerness House after their rural estate.

6 Greenwall, Holm, Mainland　　　　　　　　HY 515014

Private.

This well-preserved house was built in 1656 for Patrick Graham, the second son of Bishop George Graham, who came to Orkney from Dunblane in 1615. It has two storeys plus an attic, and the gables are crowstepped in the fashion of the time. The main entrance is elaborated with a stone porch, and above it there is a worn stone that was probably originally carved with a coat of arms.

In the nineteenth century there was some alteration to the house, and various farm buildings were added.

7 Earl's Palace, Birsay, Mainland　　　　　　HY 248277

Historic Scotland; signposted.

This palace was built about 1574 by Earl Robert Stewart, father of Earl Patrick and half-brother to Mary, Queen of Scots. Today it is very ruinous and it can be hard to imagine its former glory, but early drawings show a fine Renaissance building around a central courtyard surrounded by gardens as well as greens for bowling and for archery.

The palace was of two storeys, with higher towers at three

Figure 54. The Earl's Palace at Birsay, from the Rev. Barry's *History*, published in 1805.

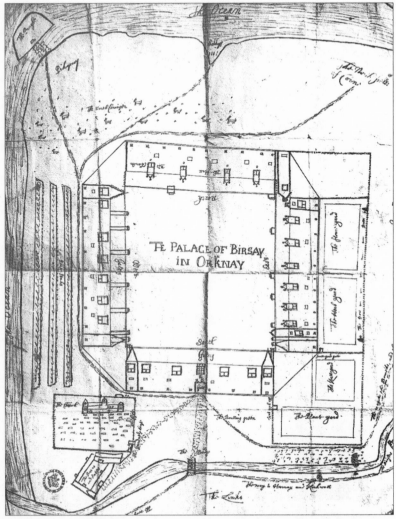

Figure 55. The Earl's Palace, Birsay; detailed seventeenth-century plan of the Earl's Palace at Birsay in its heyday. There are flower, herb and vegetable gardens to the east, bordered by archery butts, and three long peat stacks for the winter to the west. the church lies to one side of the main entrance, with a bowling green to the other. The bedchamber is noted in the north wing, and between the palace and the Brought of Birsay a herd of deer have been drawn.

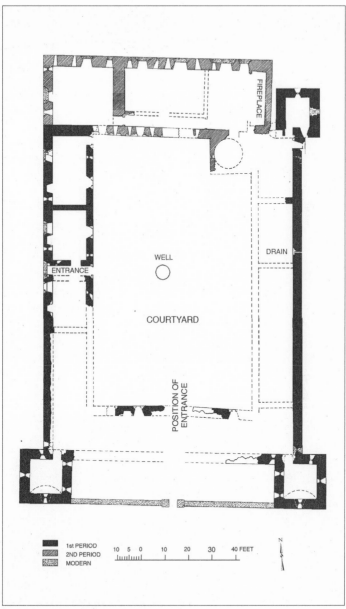

Figure 56. The Earl's Palace, Birsay.

corners and a well in the inner courtyard. It was well designed for defence with gun loops facing outwards for security, though on the north and east wings the windows of the upper floor were ornamented with carvings. There was one main entrance into the courtyard, and even the interior was protected by gun loops facing inwards. The ground floors contained a kitchen and many stores, most of which opened directly on to the courtyard. Above these were the domestic quarters of the earl and his retainers. Inside it seems that it was not quite so austere as the preoccupation with defence might suggest. A description of 1633 recounts painted scenes from the Bible, which decorated the interior and describes the building as 'sumptuous and stately'.

Over the entrance gateway Earl Robert placed his coat of arms together with an inscription that was later to get the family into trouble. The inscription read '*Dominus Robertus Stuartus filius Jacobi Quinti Rex Scotorum hoc opus instruxit*' and it contains an important grammatical error because it uses the wrong form of *Rex* – King. As written, the translation is: 'Lord Robert Stewart, King of the Scots, son of James the Fifth, erected this building'; were *Regis* to have been used correctly instead it would have read: 'Lord Robert Stewart, son of James the Fifth, King of the Scots, erected this building.' When Earl Robert's son Patrick was tried in Edinburgh he was charged, among other things, with not removing this treasonable inscription. His defence was that it was a simple grammatical mistake (but he was still executed, though not for his grammar alone).

8 St Magnus Church, Birsay, Mainland   HY 247277

Opposite the Earl's Palace.

The present church dates to the second half of the seventeenth century, but this is an ancient Christian site. It is thought that Earl Thorfinn's Norse minster was situated here, and prior to the foundation of St Magnus in Kirkwall, Birsay was the seat of the Bishopric of Orkney and an important centre of administration and religious power. After the transition of power to Kirkwall it continued to be an important place, and the foundations of a sixteenth-century Bishop's Palace may well lie close by.

Work on the present building started in 1664, and it was enlarged in 1760 with later alterations. St Magnus today is a single-storey building, though an illustration by George Low in 1771 shows that it then had two floors with an external stair. The present structure contains many fragments from the earlier building works, including a blocked door and the belfry, which dates to the seventeenth century, as well as a small lancet window with the inscription 'S Bellus' on the sill which is a reference to the medieval Bishop's Palace that was situated here.

9 Rendall Dovecote, Mainland   HY 422207

OIC.

This dovecot was built in the seventeenth century to provide meat and eggs for the family living in the nearby Hall of Rendall. Four projecting courses of flagstone run round the outside of the circular walls in order to stop rats from climbing into the structure to attack the birds and steal the eggs. The birds entered through the roof and there are nesting boxes inside, formed by gaps between the stones.

10 Breckness House, Mainland   HY 224093

Private; footpath along the coast from Stromness.

Breckness House was built in 1633 for Bishop George Graham. It is now ruined, but it is possible to get an idea of its former grandeur, though some decorated stonework has been removed for use elsewhere.

11 The Old Storehouse, St Mary's,   HY 477 013
Holm, Mainland

Private.

This store was built in 1649 to receive the goods that local farmers paid in lieu of rent. In 1694 it was attacked and emptied by French pirates. In addition to storing goods it has been used to house the cargos from local shipwrecks and it was also used for the herring trade.

Figure 57.
The porch and doorway into Breckness House, drawn in the nineteenth century.

12 Dishan Tower, Shapinsay   HY 479165

Private.

This tower was built in the seventeenth century as a dovecot, but in the nineteenth century it was converted into a salt-water shower. It is an elaborate structure: a round tower topped with a castellated parapet and a rectangular cap-house with crow-stepped gables.

13 Tofts, Quandale, Rousay   HY 373326

Private; on Rousay Heritage Walk.

This building is very ruinous, but it has been documented back as far as 1601, and it is one of the oldest two-storey houses in Orkney. It would have been the main house of the township of Quandale, which was cleared of its inhabitants in 1845 so that the landlord could graze sheep.

14 Langskaill House, Gairsay   HY 434219

Private.

There has been a house at Langskaill at least since Norse times, for it was here that Svein Asleifarson, one of the more famous Orcadian

Norsemen, had his hall. In 1588 Gairsay was sold by William Muir-head to William Bannatyne, and it is recorded that there was a 'maner place' on the island at the time: it has been suggested that this can be identified as the basis of the eastern range of the present building at Langskaill. Nevertheless, most of the present house dates to 1676, when it was built for Sir William Craigie, who had recently married Margaret Honeyman, daughter of the Bishop of Orkney.

Originally, the house ran around three sides of a courtyard, with a screen wall and central entrance on the fourth. On either side of the entrance were gun loops out to sea. The house combined elements of defence with comfort: times were still uncertain in the seventeenth century. Langskaill has undergone several alterations, and today it is much reduced in size. Only the screen wall and the eastern range of buildings survive, but it is still an elegant dwelling which retains many seventeenth-century features.

The gateway still bears an elaborate armorial panel, and the initials of William and Margaret, for whom the house was built, are carved over the eastern entrance.

15 Carrick House, Eday   HY 566384
Private.

The original house at Carrick was built in the early sixteenth century for John Stewart, Lord Kinclaven, who was another of Earl Robert Stewart's sons. This house was sited right by the sea, and the main entrance was a gateway designed for visitors arriving by boat. Since John Stewart's time the house has gone through many changes of ownership, and it has been much enlarged. It became famous in the early eighteenth century, when the Orkney pirate John Gow led an attack on the house and was captured after his ship, the *Revenge*, ran aground nearby on the Calf of Eday. Gow's career was short: he was held captive in Carrick House and then sent to London where he was tried and executed, but he has since been immortalised by Sir Walter Scott, who used his story as the basis for his novel *The Pirate*.

In 1662, one Arthur Buchanan and his wife Marjory Buxton came into possession of Carrick House and their initials are

Figure 58. Carrick House in Eday, a nineteenth-century view and detail of the carved stone over the entrance.

inscribed on the armorial panel over the gate. They also had property in Shapinsay, and an elaborate gateway still bearing their initials may be seen in the grounds of Balfour Castle.

16 Saltworks, Calf of Eday   HY 574391 & 575387

Private; boats may be arranged from Calfsound in Eday.

There are two buildings here, probably dating to the seventeenth century, built to process seawater and extract the salt. They had curved end walls which stood in the sea, and each was divided into two by a massive central wall. Each room had a fireplace opening off this wall and there is also evidence of various air vents. The back walls of the buildings were dug into the slope of the shore, and above them lie the remains of a mound, which have been suggested as the traces of the fuel stack that would have fuelled them. In addition, faint traces of booths along the shore to the east of the extant buildings may provide evidence for earlier salt workings here.

Individual families would normally make salt at home by evaporating seawater in a pan over the kitchen fire. In the 1790s, however, the landlords on Eday prevented them from doing this because of the amount of peat that it used and fears that peat supplies would not last. The salt works on the Calf of Eday are recorded in 1630, when they were set up by the Earl of Carrick, and they used both turf and peat for fuel. This site is interesting because of the scale on which salt manufacture was apparently taking place. Salt could be exchanged for meal in the neighbouring islands.

17 Noltland Castle, Westray   HY 429487

Historic Scotland; signposted.

Noltland Castle was built in the late sixteenth century for Gilbert Balfour. Balfour originated from Fife, and he had a troubled history: he spent some time on a French galley after the murder of Cardinal Beaton; he was involved in the murder of Darnley; and later he was accused of treason. He had been given lands in Westray by his brother-in-law, Adam Bothwell, Bishop of Orkney, in 1560, about which time he became Sheriff of Orkney. Perhaps Balfour saw Westray as a convenient refuge, certainly the castle is surprisingly well defended: there are over 70 gun loops and the Z-plan design lent itself well to defence.

Noltland was built on a grand scale and it combines military austerity with aristocratic elegance. The ground floor is simple and was made up of storerooms and the kitchen, with the main hall and private dwellings on higher floors. Despite the emphasis on defence, Balfour also created courtly apartments for himself and his family: a broad stairway with a carved stone newel post led up to the great hall, and there are many small details that suggest that comfort was not at all forgotten. It has been described as 'a smart house sitting on top of two floors of purposeful artillery fortification'.*

Despite the apparent care taken in its design, Noltland was not held successfully by the Balfours. On two occasions it fell into the hands of the Stewart earls, with whom the Balfours were quarrelling. Gilbert Balfour himself came to a sticky end; he continued to involve himself in political intrigue and was executed in Sweden in 1576. After his death the castle continued in use, however. It was added to by Earl Patrick Stewart, and was sold in 1606 to Sir John Arnot, Treasurer-Depute of Scotland, who was to become Sheriff

*Gifford, *The Buildings of Scotland*, p. 343.

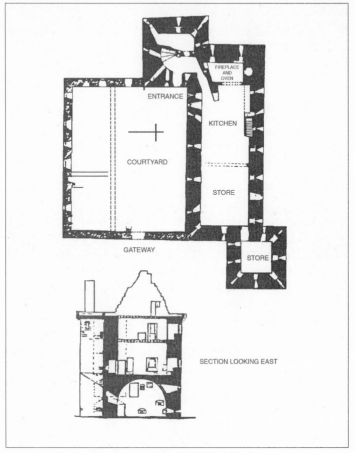

Figure 59. Nineteenth-century plans of Noltland Castle.

of Orkney in 1611.

In 1745 it was occupied by defeated Jacobite officers, as a result of which it was set on fire by their Hanoverian enemies. The castle was designed as a three-storey building, but it was never finished. Nevertheless, it was used for over 200 years and the present remains include later alterations and additions, such as the courtyard and foundations of domestic ranges, which may be seen on the south side.

Figure 60. Noltland Castle, from the Rev. Barry's *History*, published in 1805.

Figure 61. The main stair
and carved newel post of
Noltland Castle in the
nineteenth century.

The Improving Years:
Orkney in the Eighteenth and Nineteenth Centuries

Agriculture in the Eighteenth Century

After the terrible years of the sixteenth and seventeenth centuries things could only improve for the Orcadians. Improvement was slow, however, and famine was still an issue during the eighteenth century, but life gradually began to change and Orkney came more and more into contact with the British mainland as events there, largely related to the Industrial Revolution, impacted on island ways. Improved transport, both by land and sea, meant not only that goods and ideas could reach Orkney more easily, but also that it was easier and more economic to export Orcadian goods and livestock for sale in the south.

Orkney land is essentially fertile, and through the eighteenth century various landowners tried to set in place agricultural improvement schemes to repair the neglect of previous years. Some were ambitious, such as the construction of the Great Park of Cara for the management of cattle in South Ronaldsay, while others were more moderate in scale. None were very successful. In general, Orkney farms were operated on an age-old system that imposed its own restrictions on the land, such as the division of holdings into smaller and smaller properties. Some redivision of the land started in the early eighteenth century, but it did not really take off until the nineteenth century.

In many ways the eighteenth century led the way for the improvements that were to come in the following century. Communications with the south continued to improve, there was increasing employment as local industry started up, merchant ships called in to Stromness to take on water and crews, and larger-scale fishing fleets began to be seen. But, this was still a time of great hardship. Most Orcadians continued to share their traditional stone long-houses with the livestock and they worked on lands that were

Figure 62. Kirkwall in the early nineteenth century. This view is interesting because it shows the old alignment of the sea front.

divided according to the old run-rig system. Metalled roads were unknown, and wheeled transport was rare. Kirkwall was the main settlement, with trade strictly controlled; in the early eighteenth century Stromness was just a hamlet.

Nineteenth-century Farm Improvements

With the coming of the nineteenth century all this was to change, and those Orcadians who lived through the century must have seen changes almost akin to those seen by the people who lived through the following century. Agricultural improvement began to take off early in the nineteenth century: the system of run-rig was abolished and land was reallocated on longer-term rents; common land was divided (though it was often left open and used for local grazing at first); drainage was improved; settlement expanded; and the hill lands were taken into cultivation (many upland rural place-names date from this time). At the same time agricultural life was improved by new crop rotation techniques, and even new crops: potatoes were introduced into Orkney in the 1750s. Improved ferry transport meant that livestock and goods could be taken from the islands more easily for more profitable sale in the Scottish mainland.

New-fangled machinery, such as threshing machines, began to make its way to Orkney. These might be powered by wind, water, horses, or hand, but they made life much easier for the farmer and his family. Their farm buildings were also changed. In some cases this comprised a modification of the old dwelling, to introduce internal divisions and integral fireplaces, and in other cases new-style houses, quite separate from the accommodation for the animals, were built. Two-storey buildings became more common-place. Innovations such as wooden floors and flagstone roofs became common (the latter as a result of restrictions on turf-cutting and thatching). The landowners also benefited from these innovations and increased prosperity, and there was much building work. Many of the larger farms date from this time: the houses are more spacious and comfortable and they often include elaborate outbuildings to house both animals and machinery, such as horse gins. Several landowners also built large meal mills, such as Tormis-ton Mill in Stenness and Boardhouse Mill in Birsay. The tenants' grain could be milled centrally (with profit for the landowner), and gradually the small click mills went out of use. All in all, farm life was transformed through the nineteenth century.

The Kelp Industry

The changes did not only relate to agriculture, however. In the eighteenth century an industry arose burning seaweed, 'kelp', which was needed for its high alkali content by the burgeoning industries such as glass and soap manufacture further south in Britain. The first kelp burning took place in Stronsay in the 1720s, but within a few decades it had spread throughout the islands, particularly the Northern Isles, and at its peak the industry engaged about 3,000 islanders.

Men, women and children were employed on the kelp, harvest-ing the weeds, laying them out to dry, tending the kilns as the weed was burnt to a hard glassy slag, and loading it onto the boats for export. The industry was controlled by the landowners, and to them it brought great wealth, although for those who undertook the labour it was hard work that often resulted in health problems such as chest complaints, but some profit also filtered down and small luxuries such as tea and imported clothes became more commonplace throughout the isles.

The kelp industry really thrived in the period between 1770 and 1830, when access to other forms of alkali was expensive and variable during the American War of Independence and the Napoleonic Wars. In Orkney, it had great impact. The lairds were able to afford town houses in Kirkwall as well as their island homes, and businesses there thrived. Kirkwall expanded, and an account of 1813 waxes eloquently about the 'dancing assemblies and card assemblies alternately every week: and popular Lectures on Chymistry . . .'*

Out in the rural estates, many families kept large numbers of horses to help with the transport of the weed, and wheeled carts became common. Island populations remained unusually high at this time as people found work, if seasonal, at the kelp. Today, however, all that is left are the grand houses built with the wealth of the time, such as the West End Hotel in Kirkwall, a town house for Captain William Richan and his wife. In addition there are the small stone-lined hollows, kelp-kilns, where the kelp was burned. Numerous kelp-kilns litter the island coasts in any area where the kelp harvest was good, together, in some places, with the lengths of stone walling on which the weed would be spread to dry. In 1830, kelp prices plummeted and the industry collapsed; it was revived in the 1840s when it was used largely for its iodine content, but the industry never reached its previous heights, though it did continue into the 1930s.

Linen and Straw

At the same time as the kelp industry, other small industries were thriving in Orkney. From the eighteenth century, linen manufacture, relying on cheap labour and imported flax from the Baltic,

*Quoted in Gifford, *The Buildings of Scotland*, p. 311.

was encouraged by the British Linen Company and it provided work for many women. Much of the work was done at home, and it was, of course, the landlords and merchants who really profited, but it provided some financial independence to the female population of the islands. Nevertheless, by the 1830s the industry had disappeared, largely due to the impact of mechanisation further south.

With the demise of linen, straw plaiting was introduced and took over for a while, employing local women working with imported straw to make bonnets and other goods. By the mid-century, however, even the straw plaiting was on the decline (though there is still a thriving craft industry of traditional straw-backed chairs and other goods).

Fishing and Whaling

One attraction of these industries was that they provided work for the women in a society where many men were away for long periods. Orcadians have always mixed farm work with life at sea, but longer trips away became the norm for many islanders throughout the eighteenth century and into the nineteenth. This was partly a technological development as boats and navigation got better, and partly an economic one. Fishing, whaling and the Hudson's Bay Company were all to lend a hand. Fishing had, of course, always been important, but commercial fishing was a new development, started in the seventeenth century by the Dutch fleet. Gradually it took off among Orkneymen, encouraged by better transport and opening markets outwith the islands. It included both long-distance trips and local catches. Orcadians crewed many boats leaving for Iceland and Greenland, and in the early nineteenth century the seasonal herring fishing was to bring a transient population and wealth to several Orkney islands, such as Stronsay.

The herring fishing left a particular mark on Stronsay in the village of Whitehall, which was founded in the early nineteenth century as a fishing village. It is now a quiet hamlet, but it must have appeared very different at the height of the herring season, when over 400 boats would come from as far afield as south-west Scotland to work the local waters and bring their catch in for processing. The herring did not provide year-round work, but during the short six- to eight-week season, which started in late July, Whitehall would become a bustling centre with the arrival of several hundred women, who came to clean and salt the fish, as well as the coopers and numerous others who serviced the boats. All of these people had to be fed and housed, and so new buildings and temporary trades would spring up, and it is reported that there were as well many visitors who came to see the scene. Other herring centres sprang up in Stromness, Burray and South Ronaldsay and the traces may be seen in surviving stone warehouses and sheds, but none were as successful as Stronsay.

Whaling involved rather longer journeys and greater dangers, but it had been a part of Orkney life from the late eighteenth century, and at about the same time the Hudson's Bay Company also started to recruit Orcadians. Stromness was a convenient port of call for their ships before they crossed the Atlantic. It was the last place from which fresh water (from Login's Well at the south end of the town) and supplies could be obtained, and a large proportion of the Company's men were recruited from the islands. This included not only seamen: carpenters, blacksmiths, and tailors were all needed, as were clerks. Orkneymen were highly sought after because of their survival skills in the open landscape and also because of the high educational standards of the islands. From this tradition rose a few well-known names such as John Rae, who explored in the Arctic and was to be instrumental in providing information relating to the fate of the Franklin expedition. Rae went on to discover the final links to the Northwest Passage. At the same time, Orcadians also served in merchant ships and in the Royal Navy.

The foundations of Orcadian travelling had been laid down by the Norse centuries before, but they really came to fruit in these years and many rural Orcadian homes would have been quite familiar with exotic goods and stories that might have seemed much more out of place in the mainland of Britain. Earlier in the eighteenth century Orkney had played host to Cook's fleet on the return from its third voyage, by which time Cook himself had been murdered. Contrary weather meant that the fleet could not make it south to their home port, so they were forced to stay in Orkney for some weeks, during which time many of the sailors were billeted in local homes. As they were short of money, payment for this hospitality was made in exotic goods and souvenirs brought back from the South Seas, some of which may be seen in the Stromness Museum, while others are still to be found in private houses.

Trade and Defence in Peace and War

At home, Kirkwall suffered from the abrupt drop in income of the landlords with the decline of the kelp and linen industries. Its importance, however, had already been under attack. Stromness, hardly a hamlet before the eighteenth century, had risen in importance as the convenient watering place for trans-Atlantic trade and as it grew in size and wealth, so the local merchants wished for the same rights of free trade that the merchants of Kirkwall enjoyed. In 1742, the Stromness traders took Kirkwall to court over their taxes, and eventually they won the rights they needed: there were now two towns to compete for the economic wealth of the islands. Much of the building in Stromness dates to this time.

Abroad, the nineteenth century was not only a time of great technological and industrial development, but also of war, and this had its own impact in Orkney. Not only were local industries, such as the kelp, encouraged as a result of the problems of trading in areas where aggression was rife, but there were also more direct impacts on the landscape. Around the sound of Longhope in Hoy, Martello towers were built to provide a protected base for convoys of merchant ships setting out to cross the North Sea. The North Sea and Atlantic crossings had became dangerous due to action by the United States Navy in retaliation for action by British vessels against those who traded with Napoleon and his allies. Although they were never actually needed for naval defence, the towers continued in active service throughout the two World Wars. The tower at Hackness is now in State care and may be visited.

A Developing Cultural Life

This period of expansion and innovation benefited not only the economic life of the islanders; there was also a general upswing in cultural life. Kirkwall had long had a grammar school – the earliest records of the school date to the 1540s, when a Thomas Houston was appointed master by Bishop Robert Reid – but its origins may go back to the Norse period, to a church school founded by Bishop Bjarni in the twelfth century. Throughout the nineteenth century, however, improved economics combined with current legislation to increase the facilities for and uptake of education throughout the isles. There was also much church building in rural parishes, and libraries, too, became more commonplace. In this field Kirkwall had also led the way: the public library here was founded in 1683 (records suggest that there was an existing library at this time). In this academic atmosphere it was not surprising that other institutions flourished. *The Orcadian* newspaper was founded in 1854, and though it was not the first to deal with local affairs, it was the first truly local publication: previous publications had all been based in Edinburgh.

At this time, with the opening-up of transport across Britain, Orkney attracted many distinguished visitors, such as the novelist Walter Scott. The nineteenth century saw the start of the great British traditions of tourism and travel, and Orkney played an important role in this. Queen Victoria was to open British eyes to the attractions of Scotland in general, and the romantic and inquisitive nature that was commonplace at the time would benefit from the lure of more remote and distinct places such as St Kilda and Orkney. The first picture postcards of Orkney appeared in the 1880s and they provide a fascinating glimpse of the islands at this time.

Orkney was a popular place to visit, with its wealth of ancient ruins and its spectacular land and seascapes, and its specific attractions were further promoted by Sir Walter Scott. He journeyed round the islands in 1814 and had both antiquarian and historical interests. He subsequently used many of the well-known sites in his popular novel *The Pirate*, which was based on the story of the eighteenth-century Orkney pirate John Gow, and set in Orkney and Shetland, with the finale at the Stones of Stenness. In common with much of Scott's work, prominence is given in the novel to the general landscape of archaeological monuments that then survived and this did much to draw popular attention to the interest and attractions of the ancient ruins both in Orkney and elsewhere. Scott was not the only literary visitor and other accounts of Orkney flourished.

All in all it is not surprising that so many writers and poets have come from or been influenced by Orkney. Literature, learning and the arts are part of an old tradition (perhaps as far back as the Orkneyinga Saga), but one which thrived in the nineteenth century and continues to this day. Visitors to the islands have each formed different opinions on their stay, and each has left behind their own particular account, but there was also a solid foundation of local talent and production. As a part of this great cultural tradition it is fitting, in a book like this, to mention the academic discipline of antiquarianism, which flourished in the islands at this time.

The archaeological record of Orkney was already well known by the nineteenth century. There had been 'excavations' at least as far back as the Norse period when Maeshowe and other tombs were opened, but the first controlled investigation of a site may be said to have taken place under the direction of Sir Joseph Banks at the Bay of Skaill, near to Skara Brae (which had not yet been discovered). It is not surprising that monuments that were so visible as the upstanding stones and cairns of Orkney should attract interest, and in 1805 the Reverend George Barry provides descriptions of several sites in his *History of the Orkney Islands*:

'The island of Westray, in particular, contains, on the north and south-west sides of it, a great number of graves, scattered over two extensive plains, of that nature which are called links in Scotland. They have at first, perhaps, been covered by tumuli, or barrows, though of this there is no absolute certainty, as the ground, on which they are, is composed entirely of sand, by the blowing of which the graves have been only of late discovered.'*

The Orkney Antiquarian Society was not to be formed until the early 1920s, but early interest in the monuments came from both locals and further afield and there was a Natural History Society from the early nineteenth century. Archaeological work in the nineteenth century included both excavation and survey and was of varying degrees of success in terms of the collection of scien-

---

*Barry, G., *History of the Orkney Islands* (1805) (Edinburgh: Mercat Press, 1975), p. 205.

tific information. Some 'explorations' might be better classified as uncontrolled treasure hunting, but there was also much good work by local antiquarians, such as George Petrie. The results of his excavations are still of use today and information from the islands was included in many great studies, such as those of the Edinburgh antiquarian Daniel Wilson and London archaeologist John Evans. This work was not only of local interest; Orkney, with its rich archaeological heritage, was of great importance in the development of archaeology as a discipline both in Scotland and beyond. Archaeologists came from far afield to study the sites and finds. This is a role which has been maintained right to the present day. Many archaeologists still visit Orkney frequently, and in recent decades Orkney has become home to a thriving community of those who make their livelihood from the past: archaeologists; custodians; lecturers; tourist guides and so on. Information from Orcadian sites still plays an important role in the development of archaeological theory and interpretation today.

EIGHTEENTH- AND NINETEENTH-CENTURY SITES (see map, p. xxxi)

Eighteenth- and nineteenth-century sites include many fine churches and chapels too numerous to mention here. In addition, there are many private homes, both grand and small, which are typical of the developments of this time. The entries below have been included in an attempt to pick out a few representative buildings to give an idea of life in Orkney during these centuries.

1 Town Hall, Kirkwall, Mainland   HY 448109

OIC; in centre of town.

Kirkwall Town Hall was built in 1884 by the Orkney architect Thomas Peace. At the time it contained the library and post office, as well as a hall and council chambers and offices. It is a typical example of the nineteenth-century Baronial style thought fitting for a centre of such civic dignity.

2 Ayre Mills, Kirkwall, Mainland   HY 446113

Private.

These mills date back to the nineteenth century when the mouth of the Oyce was open and the tidal flow could be used for power. With time, water power was replaced by steam, but the central location was a good one for local industry. Originally there was a saw mill here, but in later life it was a meal mill. Milling ceased in 1940 and, after a brief period as a barracks in the mid-twentieth century, it was used for egg grading and packing by the Orkney Egg Producers Ltd. Industrial use halted in the 1970s and the building has been partially converted into dwellings.

3 West End Hotel, 14 Main Street,   HY 447105
Kirkwall, Mainland

Private.

This house was built in 1824 for Captain William Richan of Rapness. It achieved notoriety as the location of a wager undertaken by Captain Richan's wife who, in a competition to consume the most expensive breakfast, is said to have placed a £50 note between slices of bread and eaten it!

4 Highland Park Distillery, Kirkwall, Mainland   HY 448096

Private; signposted; car park; visitor centre.

The distillery complex was established out of an illicit still in 1798 and extended throughout the nineteenth century. It is a typical example of the small-scale industry that flourished in Orkney at this time, helped by increasing prosperity (and legislation). Highland Park is the most northerly malt whisky distillery in the world.

5 Binscarth House, Finstown, Mainland   HY 348142

Private. Access to the woodland from Finstown.

Binscarth was built in 1850 for the Scarth family. The estate buildings include a nineteenth-century farm steading, built with all contemporary conveniences. Binscarth is known for one of

Orkney's larger plantations of woodland, clearly visible on the north side of the main road as it leaves Finstown on the way to Stromness. A footpath through the woods is especially popular during bluebell season.

6 Tormiston Mill, Stenness, Mainland   HY 319125
Historic Scotland; signposted; car park.

Tormiston Mill was built in the mid-nineteenth century as a meal mill. It comprises three storeys, with an iron water-wheel and a stone aqueduct to control the water. Today Tormiston Mill has been converted into a small visitor centre used mainly by those who wish to access Maeshowe. There is a display relating to Orkney archaeology and history, as well as a small shop, and the machinery that worked the mill may still be seen inside. Outside, the wheel and mill lade have been restored.

7 Mossetter Farm, Finstown, Mainland   HY 390197
Private.

Mossetter was immortalised by Eric Linklater as the home of Magnus Merriman in his eponymous novel. Today it is a roofless ruin, but it incorporates many features typical of the traditional farm steadings. It was built in the eighteenth century as a longhouse into which animals and people entered by the same door: the cattle turned left into the byre which lay downhill, while the family turned right, uphill into the dwelling quarters, which comprised two rooms.

The kitchen lies at the centre of the house, it was later divided and it is interesting in that it contains neuk-beds built into a projecting outshot on the far wall. These stone cupboard-like bed recesses provided a snug sleeping place and similar features have been found incorporated into some of Orkney's prehistoric buildings, such as the early houses at Skara Brae or the broch at Midhowe. In Eric Linklater's novel one of the Mossetter neuk-beds is occupied by Johnny, the hired hand, though they would originally have been used by the family. Other recesses in the kitchen walls were built to house a water barrel and for a goose to have her nest.

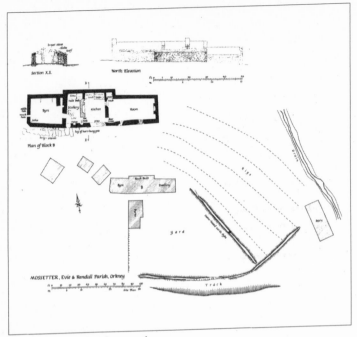

Figure 63. Mossetter farmstead.

8 Corrigall Farm, Mainland

HY 324193

OIC; signposted; car park.

The earliest buildings at Corrigall date to the mid-eighteenth century, but in line with agricultural developments they have seen much change over the years. The dwelling house was originally a typical stone and turf-roofed longhouse, with a byre for the animals at one end, but by the mid-nineteenth century it had been converted and divided into a series of rooms for the family alone. These included a parlour, an 'oot-bye' where food and drink could be stored and processed, an 'in-bye' or kitchen and living area and a bedroom. Downhill of this was a long barn and byre, with a circular kiln to dry the corn at one end, and this was later supplemented by a separate byre in which to stable the large work horses that were used in the nineteenth century. Uphill of the steading, there

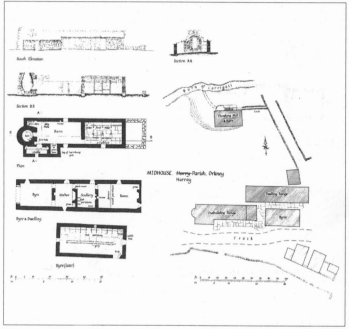

Figure 64. Corrigall farmstead.

is a burn which provided fresh water, not only for the house, but also to power a later threshing mill.

Corrigall has now been restored as a museum of nineteenth-century farming life in which many of the traditional daily tasks are demonstrated from time to time.

9 Click Mill, Dounby, Mainland   HY 325228

Historic Scotland; signposted.

This may seem a surprisingly small building for a mill, especially in comparison with the surviving Orcadian meal mills, such as Tormiston Mill, but it is typical for its type. Click mills were a common element of the smaller farmsteadings; they may have origins in the Norse period and were once much more common in both Orkney and Shetland. They went out of use with the introduction of larger central mills by the landowners in the nineteenth century. These offered economies of scale, but required payment for the service of milling. In contrast with the large meal mills, click mills have a small, horizontally set water-wheel that is connected directly to the upper mill stone. They get their name from the characteristic clicking sound of the machinery that fed the grain from a small hopper into the millstones.

This mill was built about 1823, and today it has been restored for visitors. It runs on an artificially piped supply of water, because the original burn was disturbed by road-building operations in the 1920s. Originally mills such as this would have had timber channels leading from stone-lined lades to direct the water under the mill and past the wheel. The Click Mill is recorded to have ground about a bushel (*c.* 250 kg) of grain per hour.

10 Holodyke, Harray, Mainland HY 307201

Private.

The apparently grand house of Holodyke had humble beginnings as a simple rural cottage, which was extended and converted to a schoolhouse in the mid-nineteenth century. By 1888 it had gone out of use, and it was bought by Sir Thomas Clouston as a holiday home. He added an upper floor, and later on a wing to house a dining room, as well as a crow-stepped tower over the entrance. Clouston's father was an Orcadian, but he himself moved to Edinburgh to work, where he became superintendent of the Asylum in Morningside. His Orcadian roots show up in his antiquarian interests.

11 Kirbuster Farm, Mainland HY 282254

OIC, signposted, car park.

Kirbuster has a lintel stone dated to 1723, but it has been suggested that this may mark a marriage or refurbishment of the house, so that the buildings may well date from earlier. It is unique: the only surviving example of a firehouse, a dwelling that was once common throughout northern Europe where the hearth lies in the centre of the main room. It was clearly a cut above the average steading of

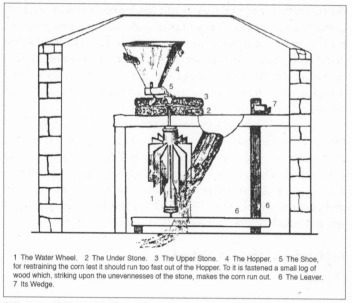

1 The Water Wheel. 2 The Under Stone. 3 The Upper Stone. 4 The Hopper. 5 The Shoe, for restraining the corn lest it should run too fast out of the Hopper. To it is fastened a small log of wood which, striking upon the unevennesses of the stone, makes the corn run out. 6 The Leaver. 7 Its Wedge.

Figure 65. A click mill, drawn by Low in 1774.

the time because it is both a more spacious and well-lit dwelling, and, unusually for the day, the animals were housed in separate buildings. The dwelling house is particularly interesting because it still retains the large central kitchen with a central fireplace, set against an upright stone fire-back, and a neuk-bed built into the thickness of the stone wall. Outside there are various buildings, including a barn with a corn-drying kiln, as well as a pigsty, and a forge. There is a small formal garden and an area of woodland which would have provided resources for home remedies together with kitchen crafts.

12 Boardhouse Mill, Birsay, Mainland   HY 254274

OIC; car park.

The three-storey Boardhouse Mill was built in 1873, and is the only watermill in Orkney still in operation. Today it grinds bere (barley) meal, for use in bannocks and other baking. This mill is the most recent of three on the site and it is the most impressive, but the other two are still in good condition, though not operational. Boardhouse was a large farmsteading and the buildings included a water-driven threshing mill, which may still be seen, as well as an earlier meal mill.

13 Fishermen's Huts, Sand Geo, Marwick HY 228234

Private, on coastal path, care needed.

Huts such as these may go back much earlier, but they were certainly in use in the nineteenth century when they were used to store gear and for overnight stays by local fishermen. The remains of rusting winches may be seen, used to draw the boats up to safety during the stormy winter months.

14 Fishermen's Huts and Boat Nousts, HY 260286
Skipi Geo, Birsay

A small turf-roofed hut stands amidst an impressive collection of boat nousts, artificially constructed hollows used to provide shelter for fishing boats during the rough winter conditions.

15 Skaill House, Sandwick, Mainland HY 234186

Signposted; car park; a joint ticket is available with Skara Brae.

The oldest ranges of the present building at Skaill House date back to the early seventeenth century. Since then there have been many additions to create what has been described as Orkney's finest ancient mansion. As seen today, Skaill is a large complex of separate wings, linked by passages and screen walls, and with a central courtyard. Although it lies near to the sea today, originally the coast lay further from the house so that, in contrast to many other 'coastal' mansions, it does not seem to be particularly orientated towards the sea.

Documents going back as far as 1492 show that there was an earlier settlement on the site, but there is no evidence for this, though in 1996, during work to prepare Skaill House for visitors, a number of skeletons were found. Excavations showed that these dated to Pictish times and it is thought likely that they relate to other skeletons recorded during work on the house in the 1930s. It is likely that there was a Pictish cemetery here, long before the house was built, and presumably a Pictish settlement lay close by, though no trace of this has yet been found.

Skaill was originally built in the 1620s for Bishop George Graham, whose descendants were to build the houses at Greenwall and Graemeshall in Holm. The complex includes a nineteenth-century walled garden, an eighteenth-century doocot, and a Home Farm steading not far away. The estate is unusual in that it has remained in the hands of the same family over the centuries. The present laird is a descendant of Bishop Graham, who acquired the lands in 1615 when he was appointed to the bishopric.

16 Stromness Museum, Mainland   HY 253086
OIC; signposted.

This house was built in 1858 as the Town Hall. In 1837 the Orkney Natural History Society was founded, and it became the home for their collections, though it now specialises in maritime subjects as well as natural history. The displays provide an excellent introduction to the richness of Orkney culture and links with the fur trade, exploration and whaling. Upstairs, the natural history cases include one with a backdrop painted by artist Stanley Cursiter.

17 Rice Warehouse, Stromness, Mainland   HY 255094
Private.

This prominent building is a warehouse built in 1760 by James Gordon, a Stromness merchant in order to store rice. Rice was transported to Orkney from the southern American states during the war of 1756–63 before being transported to the British mainland.

18 Hall of Clestrain, Mainland   HY 295075
Private.

The Hall of Clestrain is now abandoned, but it was a fine little Georgian laird's house, built in 1769 for the Honeyman family, who were the local landowners. The story goes that they honeymooned in Edinburgh, where the new Mrs Honeyman was much taken by the New Town architecture. The Hall of Clestrain was designed with this in mind. When the Honeymans moved to other estates further south the Hall was occupied by their factor, John Rae, and his family. The explorer John Rae was born here in 1813 and the house and area provided the backdrop to his childhood familiarity with the open Orkney landscape.

19 Graemeshall, Holm, Mainland   HY 484020

Private.

Graemeshall was built in the Jacobean style by a local firm of architects in the late nineteenth century. It replaced a sixteenth-century house, Meil, which stood on the same spot and some features from the earlier buildings are incorporated into the later house, such as the main door, which had been the eastern entrance to the original courtyard. It was the home of the Graham family, who had lived at Greenwall in Holm. They changed their name to Graeme, hence the name of the house. The associated buildings include a small, plain episcopal chapel which houses some medieval grave stones from the disused old Holm Parish Church nearby.

20 Covenanters' Memorial, Deerness,   HY 572087
Mainland

Private. Footpath running from car park at HY 575077.

This monument was built in 1888 to commemorate over 200 covenantors who drowned just off the coast here when their ship went down in 1679. The Covenantors were in revolt against the Crown, and those who drowned here had been captured at Bothwell Bridge. They were to be transported to the New World for sale as slaves in Barbados, but their ship cast its moorings and was driven ashore. The crew battened down the hatches and tried to prevent the prisoners from escaping, which meant that only fifty survived (most of these were recaptured and sent into slavery).

21 St Peter's Church, South Ronaldsay ND 470909

Private.

Most of St Peter's Church dates to 1801, but it was originally built in 1642, and in 1967 it was refurbished inside to show the eighteenth-century church furnishings. Gravestones from the seventeenth and eighteenth century may be found in the churchyard.

22 Martello Tower and Battery, ND 338912
Hackness, Hoy

Historic Scotland.

This tower was built in 1815, in order to defend the vulnerable anchorage of Longhope as a base for British shipping during the Napoleonic Wars. Though it appears to be circular, the design is more sophisticated because on the seaward side the wall is twice as thick as elsewhere, in order to withstand bombardment from that direction. There is only one entrance, at first-floor level, and originally reached by a retractable wooden ladder. Inside, there was a first-floor barrack room in which the gunners could sleep, with a separate cubicle for the officer in charge. There were stores and magazines below, and the gun emplacements were above. The foundations contained a water cistern, from which water could be pumped to the living quarters.

In 1866, the gun mounting was enhanced, but the tower was never actually needed for defence. Enemy ships restricted their attacks to the open sea and the guns were only fired once, in peacetime in 1892. During the First World War the tower served as a naval signal post.

Besides the Martello Tower is the battery. It was originally designed to house eight 24-pounder guns set behind an embankment and a stone parapet, but in 1866 it was modified to house four 68-pounders and the defences were strengthened. The buildings associated with the battery included a magazine for powder and arms, and a barracks.

Another Martello Tower was built on the other side of Longhope at Crock Ness to complete the defences of the bay, and it may still be seen today though it is not open to the public.

23 Melsetter House, Hoy

Private; visits may be arranged by appointment; details from Visit Orkney.

Melsetter was built at the turn of the century, in 1898, by the well-known architect William Lethaby. It was built for a wealthy Birmingham businessman, Thomas Middlemore, and his wife, and it incorporated the original buildings from an earlier house, which dated back to the early eighteenth century. It is a very fine example of an Arts and Crafts house, and combines many local materials and traditions, such as Caithness flagstones and crow-stepped gables, together with the modern ideals of the day.

The Middlemores were friends of William Morris and his wife, and many of the furnishings and decorations came from their workshop and the studios of others in their circle.

To the south-east of the entrance courtyard Lethaby added a small chapel in 1900. The estate also comprises other buildings designed by Lethaby and built at the same time.

24 Craa Nest Museum, Rackwick, Hoy

Private.

This steading house was built in the early eighteenth century and is the oldest building in Rackwick. It is presently roofed with thatch held down by heather ropes, 'simmans', overlying local flagstones. It was last used as a dwelling in 1940, but retains many original features such as box beds, flag floors and an open fire. There is also a barn with a kiln to dry oats and a byre with flagstone stalls for the animals. The steading is now open as a museum of rural life.

25 Betty Corrigall's Grave

Footpath.

Betty Corrigall lived in Hoy in the late eighteenth century and fell pregnant to a local man who ran away to sea. In common with the social conventions of the time she suffered considerable shame and was eventually successful in killing herself. As a suicide she was buried on unconsecrated ground on the boundary between the parishes of Hoy and North Walls. The grave remained unmarked for many years, until discovered by peat cutters in the 1930s. It became something of an attraction for the servicemen during the war and was eventually provided with the present picket fence in 1949, though the headstone was not erected until 1976.

26 Cantick Head Lighthouse, South Walls, Hoy

ND 346894

Private.

The lighthouse at Cantick Head was designed by the Stevensons in 1858. The tower is of brick, painted white, but it has a corbelled stone walkway below the lantern. The lighthouse complex is incorporated within a stone wall and includes a double range of keepers' houses and stores as well as an octagonal building that housed a foghorn between 1913 and 1987.

27 Sands Motel, Burray

ND 472954

Private.

This was built in 1860 as a herring store and processing house. Burray was one of several Orkney settlements that flourished during the herring boom in the nineteenth century; others included Stromness, Whitehall, Stronsay and St Margaret's Hope. The annual arrival of the herring boats, together with people to process the catch on shore, led to the construction of many buildings, not only for processing but also to house the workers. The building is now a hotel and pub.

28 Balfour Castle and Village, Shapinsay

ND 474164

Private; details of visits available from Visit Orkney.

Balfour Castle was begun in 1847, designed by the well-known architect David Bryce for the Balfour family, who had recently purchased the whole island. In common with many other buildings of the same period, it incorporated earlier dwellings within its make-up. It is a grand building in Scottish Baronial style, and has a square castellated main tower, as well as several smaller towers and turrets, some of which have steep conical roofs, while other roofs are pyramid-shaped. There are plenty of battlements and mullioned windows to provide a romantic medieval air, and this theme is carried into the inside, much of which was designed along a Jacobean style. Balfour Castle is a good example of a rare calendar house, originally designed with seven turrets, twelve doors and 365 window panes.

Colonel Balfour also had designs outwith his domestic residence. During the mid-nineteenth century he 'improved' Shapinsay generally, laying out a network of straight roads and a new field grid, as well as creating a new, planned settlement, called Balfour Village, for his workers. This village was sited on the location of the previous village of Shoreside, which had been built in the late eighteenth century. It included housing, as well as a smithy, an elaborate gateway, and an imposing gasworks in the form of a round tower. The gasworks tower has a corbelled parapet of red brick and appears to be fortified, but this is all part of the medieval illusion that Balfour wished to create. He went even further: incorporated into the structure of the tower are three carved stones, said to have been removed from Noltland Castle on Westray.

Just to the side of the pier lie the public toilets, incorporated by Balfour for the convenience of the inhabitants of the village and notable for the use of a tidal flush to clear them out twice a day.

29 Westness House, Rousay   HY 383289

Private; on Rousay Heritage Walk.

Westness House was built in the late eighteenth century and originally it was the principal house of Rousay, before the Burroughs family, who then owned the estate, built a grander dwelling at Trumland House in the 1870s. The site at Westness is one of some ancient activity; excavations have revealed a variety of Norse remains including a cemetery and a church close by, and in the twelfth century it is recorded as the main household of Rousay.

30 Trumland House, Rousay   HY 428277

Private.

Trumland House was built in the 1870s by the same architect as Balfour Castle's, David Bryce. It is a three-storey mansion in the Scottish Jacobean style, though it is a less ostentatious building than Balfour Castle. The policies include a gateway, leading to the kitchen garden, into which various ancient architectural fragments have been incorporated. These include bits of sculptured stones which are thought to come from St Mary's Church and the Wirk nearby, though some may originally have come from Kirkwall as off-cuts and spares from the building of St Magnus Cathedral in the thirteenth century.

Trumland House was almost completely destroyed by fire in the 1980s but it is currently undergoing restoration. The house was originally surrounded by fine gardens and woodland which have now been restored and enhanced and are open to the public.

31 Kelp Pits, Rousay   HY 374296

Private; on Rousay Heritage Walk.

Groups of kelp pits lie around many Orkney shores. They comprise shallow, stone-lined hollows in which seaweed, 'kelp', was burned so that the residue could be exported. Harvesting and processing the kelp provided work throughout the eighteenth century and on into the nineteenth century, and helped to keep island populations high.

32 Kelp Pits, Lamb Ness,   HY 690215
  Stronsay

Private; coastal walk to site.

By the narrow neck of the promontory of Lamb Ness lie a group of kelp pits, together with the dry-stone walls over which the kelp was dried.

33 Kelp Pits, Grice Ness, Stronsay
HY 670281

Private.

Stronsay was one of the principal centres for kelp making. Around the shoreline of Grice Ness it is possible to see the well-preserved stances on which the kelp was dried, as well as the pits in which it was burned. There is also a ruined cottage which, it has been suggested, may have housed the kelpers.

34 Kelp Pits, Latan, Stronsay
HY 631222

Private.

On the shore here there are a group of kelp pits, together with a kiln.

35 Ortie Village, Sanday
HY 686452

Private.

At least six dwellings, together with outhouses, make up this deserted village site. Ortie was built in the nineteenth century during the height of the kelp industry. Over sixty people lived here in its heyday. The ruins are interesting for the traditional construction techniques that may be seen, including roofs thatched with simmans (straw or heather ropes).

36 Scar, Sanday
HY 670451

Private.

Scar was a prosperous nineteenth-century farm where various agricultural improvements were carried out early on. The present farm complex was built in the early nineteenth century and is particularly interesting because of the arrangements made for the industrialisation of some of the everyday farm work. There was a steam-powered meal mill, the boiler-house and chimney of which may still be seen today, as well as a stone windmill, of which only a stump survives. The farm buildings include a doocot and a walled garden. The main house reflects the wealth of the early nineteenth-century farmers: it is a large building with two storeys and an attic with windows.

37 Stove, Sanday HY 609356

Private.

Stove was one of the first farms to mechanise the processes of farm work. The steading was built in the nineteenth century and included a boiler-house with chimney to provide power for a steam-driven threshing machine. Today it is ruinous.

38 Warsetter, Sanday HY 630378

Private.

The main steading at Warsetter was built in the nineteenth century, but to the east of the buildings is a large doocot with an interesting semicircular roof of flagstones which slope up to a single gable end. The doocot was probably built in the eighteenth century, though it incorporates a datestone dating to 1613 in the gable. It has been suggested that this was moved from an earlier house which stood nearby.

39 Start Point Lighthouse, Sanday HY 786435

Private, on a tidal island.

The lighthouse at Start Point was originally built in 1802 as a tower with a great stone ball on top. It was designed to be used during daylight only, but in 1806 it was converted into a night-light by the addition of a lantern with a clockwork mechanism to make it revolve. The present brick tower was built in 1870, but the keepers' quarters are original. In 1814 Sir Walter Scott visited the lighthouse and wrote that the keepers lived in greater style than that of his own house at Abbotsford in the Scottish Borders. The lighthouse is most striking today because of its decoration: it is painted in vertical bands of black and white so that it truly sticks out in the low seascapes of the eastern islands.

40 Noup Head Lighthouse,   HY 392500
Westray

Private; care needed on high cliffs.

The lighthouse at Noup Head was built by David Stevenson in 1898 in brick. It is well worth a visit for its spectacular location and seabird colonies.

41 Dennis Head Lighthouse and Beacon,   HY 790553
North Ronaldsay

Private.

Dennis Head was one of the earliest lighthouses in Scotland, and the first in the Northern Isles. It was built in 1789, and the remains comprise the ruins of the original housing for the keepers, as well as the tower. In 1809, the original light was replaced by a great masonry ball, which had originally been atop the beacon at Start Point in Sanday. By that stage, the alteration of the Sanday lighthouse had rendered the light in North Ronaldsay less important. Nevertheless, in 1852, a new lighthouse was commissioned, about a kilometre away. This was designed in brick by Alan Stevenson, and it is the tallest land-based lighthouse in Britain (41 metres tall). It is visually striking, because it is painted in wide red and white horizontal stripes to aid its identification from sea amongst the low Northern Isles.

42 Sheep Dyke,   HU 7654
North Ronaldsay

This stone dyke was built in the nineteenth century to encircle the island and confine the sheep to the foreshore. North Ronaldsay sheep are a unique breed, and feed mainly on seaweed. The dyke measures 19 km, and the island system includes various pounds, or punds, where the sheep could be gathered at various times of the year. Work on the dyke was originally set up as a measure to cope with the general unemployment of the time, but it is still functioning as a sheep dyke and kept in good repair today.

North Ronaldsay also contains two dykes built of earth which divide the island into three parts. These dykes are known as the Matches Dyke and the Muckle Gairsay. They are marked on a map of the late eighteenth century so they must be earlier than the stone sheep dyke, but their age is unknown though it has been suggested they may even be prehistoric in origin.

War and Peace:
From the Twentieth to the Twenty-first Century

If the nineteenth century saw great changes to life in Orkney, the twentieth century was to see even greater. At first the process was mainly a consolidation of that which had run before. Agriculture continued to prosper and improving communications worked to maintain Orkney within the mainstream of British life. But there was to be an added impetus to change in this century. The strategic importance of Orkney led to great activity during both World Wars, and the arrival of so many outside personnel was to have its own implications. Not only were new ways and customs introduced, but a whole infrastructure also had to be developed, from roads to entertainment and food supplies. The end of the Second World War left Orkney once again to its own devices, but things could never be the same again. Orkney was not to be allowed to drift, either. In the 1970s another technological revolution arrived with the introduction of the oil industry to Orkney.

Into the twenty-first century the addition of broadband internet services to the suite of improved communications made Orkney a desirable place to live and so the island population has continued to flourish. There are two Higher Education Institutions: Orkney College, part of the University of the Highlands and Islands; and the International Centre for Island Technology, part of Edinburgh's Heriot Watt University. Orkney is an important visitor destination, there is a thriving artistic and craft community, and the archipelago has once more come to the fore, this time as a leader in the field of renewable energy. While the oil industry still thrives, the potential of the islands for wind and wave power has led to the arrival of new professionals. The establishment of the European Marine Energy Centre as a focus for the development and testing of wave and tidal generation demonstrates that Orkney still has an exciting future in the establishment of appropriate technologies.

Agriculture

Agriculture remains a mainstay of life in Orkney. At the beginning of the century it followed much the same pattern that had been set in the previous years. There was slowly increasing mechanisation, and new crops and techniques were still being introduced. Tractors began to be used prior to the First World War, though they did not become commonplace until after the Second, and the introduction of wild white clover improved crop rotation and pasture. As a result the numbers of cattle could be increased and the farmers' reliance on less secure crops of cereals began to diminish. At first the cattle were used largely for dairying and so the local butter and cheese industries flourished, but from the 1970s European regulations have led to a switch to predominantly beef herds. As farming prospered, estate sizes continued to grow and farm dwellings and outbuildings were improved. During the 1930s, when the rest of Britain was suffering a depression, agriculture in Orkney thrived and was held up as an example to the rest of the country.

One offshoot of the farming culture was the egg industry, which was particularly important in Orkney throughout the mid-twentieth century. Large wooden sheds were erected for the hens and eggs were exported across Britain. This industry was hard hit by a great gale in 1952 which destroyed many of the hen houses, and it finally declined in the 1960s with the increasing costs of transportation and competition from battery farming in the south. The decline of the egg industry affected not only the producers, but there was also a knock-on effect as many rural shops lost business. Local sales of poultry food disappeared and wider social implications began to be felt.

Despite this set-back agriculture continues to thrive and now involves not just the production of basic staples but also of a wide variety of foods. The food producers of Orkney have worked hard to develop a name for quality, locally-produced, goods that embraces items such as prime beef, cheese, baking, beer and seafood. Food from Orkney is exported across Britain and is much sought after in many prestigious restaurants and shops. Commercial farming of a range of seafood, including salmon, lobster and mussels, has expanded the range of Orkney products.

The Coming of War

Besides the changes in agriculture, the twentieth century saw other changes to Orcadian society on a more general level. The foundations for these were laid early on, but the real stimulus came with the two World Wars. The strategic importance of Scapa Flow had been demonstrated in the previous century, and in 1914–1918 it became the home for the Great Fleet, and with the fleet came its personnel. About 100,000 people were sent to Orkney at this time: most were billeted aboard ship, but others were billeted on shore, and of course such a great influx of people was not without repercussions. Roads were improved, there was a great boom for farmers and merchants, and off-duty staff visited the monuments and sights of Orkney. Of course, there was also a movement of local people away from the islands, as Orcadians were drafted into service elsewhere. In 1918 the first air strikes to launch from an aircraft carrier, HMS *Furious*, took place; the wartime infrastructure had, by now, expanded to include air stations for the first warplanes.

In the First World War there was little attempt to defend the great harbour of Scapa Flow, beyond the sinking of a few blockships at the entrances to make access difficult, and at the end of the war it was considered the best anchorage for the German High Seas Fleet, which had been interned. Safe it may have been, but not from within. On 21 June 1919 the ships slowly sank after the German Admiral had given orders for them to be scuttled. Even today, so many years later, the school party out for a day trip in the Flow who just happened to witness the Fleet sinking around them, is still remembered. One other event of this war, which has its place in local legend, is the sinking of HMS *Hampshire*, when she struck a mine off Marwick Head on the west coast of Mainland. On board was Lord Kitchener, the Minister for War, and people are still critical of the inadequacies of the official rescue attempt and the small part that local civilians were allowed to play. Only twelve members of the crew survived. Other notable losses of the First World War included HMS *Vanguard*, which exploded at her moorings in 1917, and HMS *Opal* and HMS *Narborough*, which ran into cliffs off South Ronaldsay in a storm in 1918.

In the Second World War the Flow was once more to play an

important role, but this time it was complemented by events on land. War had taken a new turn and now the Fleet was supplemented by air power. Four airfields were built in Orkney, and there was also a great system of coastal defence, which included lookouts and anti-aircraft positions. This time many more personnel were based on land, and the building work also included bases with dormitories, canteens and even theatres. Early on in the war a German submarine, the U-47, penetrated Scapa Flow and sank HMS *Royal Oak* with a huge loss of life. The defence of the Flow was clearly not adequate and so an ambitious plan was devised to link the Southern Isles: Lamb Holm; Glims Holm; Burray; and South Ronaldsay. Barriers would prevent seaborne craft from entering the Flow and in addition they could be metalled on top and used for traffic. The project was started during the war and carried out by prisoners, but it was not to be finished until after hostilities had ended. The Churchill Barriers, as they are known, form an important link to the Southern Isles, and they have had, of course, a great impact on life in these islands.

The Italian Chapel and Other Remains

Many of those working on the barriers were Italian prisoners of war, and in Lamb Holm lie the remains of one of their camps. Most of it is now reduced to the grass-covered concrete foundations, but amidst these rises the ornate white façade of a small chapel. All is not quite as it seems, however, for the chapel was built and decorated by the prisoners using two Nissen huts. Inside there are elaborate paintings, ironwork and carved stone. All are made from materials to hand, including driftwood and old tin cans: the painting behind the altar was copied from a religious postcard carried in his pocket by the painter Domenico Chiocchetti, and the hanging lamps are made from discarded beef tins. Outside is a fine sculpture of St George and the Dragon, worked in cement.

Since the war much of its clutter has been reduced to foundations, but there is still plenty to be seen and the wartime remains of Orkney are now recognised as being of archaeological interest in their own right. Many of the better buildings were converted for farm use, others into dwellings. Nissen huts, converted for many different uses, dot the countryside. Foundations and concrete pill-boxes mark the site of the various camps and airfields, and round the coast many defences remain. In Hoy, the old oil pumping station at Lyness has been converted into a visitor centre: a sure sign of the new archaeological respectability of these not so ancient remains.

Peacetime Visitors and Industry

In the postwar years these great changes continued, with improved communications and increasing numbers of visitors to the islands. Many southerners arrived to live in Orkney, and the population is well mixed with people from all over Britain and further afield, just as Orcadians have also left the islands to seek a life elsewhere and leave a hint of their own customs in far-off places. More visitors come as tourists.

Individual travellers to Orkney have been recording their accounts from several centuries ago (e.g. the Reverend George Low, who travelled through the islands in 1774), and the beginnings of the rise in tourism in the nineteenth century are discussed above, but mass tourism is a relatively recent concept. Surprisingly perhaps, in view of the unpredictable weather, Orkney receives large numbers of tourists each year, and these are having their own impact on the fabric of the landscape. Many former grandiose dwellings have been converted into hotels, old cottages have been spruced up for self-catering, and there are small developments of tourist cottages. The roads were greatly improved during the wars; now they must be kept up and even widened for coaches. New piers have had to be built, and the airport at Kirkwall is thriving. The advent of roll-on roll-off ferries, has meant that these developments have spread to the outer isles as well.

Archaeology provides a considerable pull for many visitors and thus the ancient heritage now provides significant economic benefit. Archaeological sites have been consolidated and laid out to receive visitors, and car parks and toilets have been built. The 'Heritage Industry' employs many people. Other tourist draws include the bird life and flora of the islands and facilities through which to appreciate them have also been upgraded. There are bird hides and many walks, as well as a wide range of information to assist the visitor. In recent years recreational diving has also added its own footprint. Not all development is related to tourism, however. In the 1970s the great oil boom spread to Orkney. Here, the physical developments are deliberately confined to the small island of Flotta, but the impact is, of course, wider. Many of those who work in Flotta live in Mainland Orkney and commute daily from Houton pier near Orphir. There has been an impact on island house prices and trade. Oil has brought added personal wealth, as well as people, but it has also brought added communal wealth to the Orkney Islands Council and this can now be played back into the fabric and well-being of the islands and their people.

The oil industry continues to flourish and has been added to by a range of businesses that exploit environmental know-how as well as the burgeoning business of renewable energy. Wind, solar and marine energy generation are all relevant to Orkney, and the skills developed here may then be exported elsewhere. Improved transport, increased wealth, and the continued influx of people have also meant that small industries can once again flourish in Orkney with confidence. The distilleries, with their respectable Orkney heritage, have been joined by two local breweries. There are silver-smiths, potters, wood turners, artists and other crafts-folk. All have left their mark in the form of workshops, visitor centres and shops.

The Culture of the Islands

If the physical side of life is active, so too is the more cultural side. Orkney has boasted several well-known artists, poets and writers, as well as composers and musicians. Some are island-born, perhaps the best known being the Stromness poet, George Mackay Brown, who has left a rich literary heritage in his poems and stories of Orkney in both modern and ancient times. Others have been attracted to move and live in the islands, such as the composer Peter Maxwell Davies. The scholarly traditions of education and literacy continue and there is perhaps more awareness of the great local resource that is available in terms of the natural and archaeo-logical history of the islands. There are local ornithologists and botanists as well as archaeologists and historians. There is no need to look far for things of interest in Orkney and this is made use of by both the tourist trade and local residents. There is now a flourishing Science Festival in Kirkwall, which offers lectures, excursions and demonstrations to visitor and resident alike, as well as a well-established Music Festival (the St Magnus Festival), and, in Stromness, the annual Folk Festival. These modern creations follow in the footsteps of a series of long-standing local events such as the annual County Show in Kirkwall, the Ba at Christmas and New Year (a football-type scrum held in the Streets of Kirkwall), and Stromness Shopping Week in July.

Children in Orkney grow up with a well-developed sense of local place and culture. They are well-versed in the history of the islands, the local dialect continues to thrive, and many take advantage of music lessons whether offered free through the local education system or projects such as the Orkney Traditional Music Project or through private enterprise such as the Wrigley School of Music.

Archaeology and the Future

The archaeological resource of the islands hardly needs to be emphasised in a book like this, and there is a great tradition of locally-based archaeological work, as well as work by those who would visit for a summer or two. In the early years of the twentieth century Gordon Childe came from Edinburgh to work on the Neolithic villages at Skara Brae in Mainland and Rinyo in Rousay, and he also spent time looking for similar sites elsewhere in the islands. At the same time, Walter Grant, a local landowner in Rousay, together with the Yorstons, a father and son who worked for his estate, worked on the excavation of several of the tombs in that island, as well as the great broch as Midhowe. This tradition continues. There are now many locally based archaeologists and they are supplemented by an annual influx of archaeologists and students. Archaeology courses leading to a degree are offered by the University of the Highlands and Islands through the Institute of Archaeology at Orkney College in Kirkwall. Excavations still take place and new sites are still discovered, from the grandiose such as Ness of Brodgar, to the humble such as the souterrain at Corrigall. Other archaeologists make a living from providing guided tours and a few have chosen to live among the rich heritage of the islands while pursuing a career that is based further south. The sites themselves form the basis for an increasing number of television programmes, magazine articles, books and internet sites, dominated perhaps by the informative *www.orkneyjar.com* site.

The archaeological record of Orkney is, in many ways, without comparison. It is a record about which there is always something more to learn. It is also a record that is constantly growing, as the landscape of today, with its tourism and energy-based developments, becomes fossilised for those who will follow us in the future. It is up to us to enjoy and to preserve it, and I hope that this book has gone a little way towards stimulating that end.

TWENTIETH-CENTURY SITES (see map, p. xxxii)

1 Hatston Airfield, Kirkwall, Mainland   HY 440110

Now an industrial estate; accessible from the main road into Kirkwall.

Hatston was in operation as a Fleet Air Arm Base during the Second World War, when it was known as HMS *Sparrowhawk*. It was the first air base in Britain to have hard tarmacadam runways. It continued in use as a civil airport for a while after the war, and the wooden huts were used for council houses. It now forms the basis of an industrial estate and some of the original buildings may still be recognised.

2 Merkister Hotel, Harray, Mainland   HY 298191

Private.

This was built as a house in 1910 for the Linklater family.

3 Twatt Airfield, Mainland   HY 260230

Private.

Twatt airfield was in use during the Second World War as a Fleet Air Arm Base, when it was known as HMS *Tern.* Though long abandoned, the remains of many concrete buildings are still extant, including the control tower and the cinema.

4 Kitchener Memorial, Marwick Head, Mainland

HY 226251

Private; footpath with car park; care needed on steep cliffs.

This square tower was built in 1924 as a memorial for the loss of HMS *Hampshire*, which was sunk by a mine off Marwick Head in June 1916. She was on her way from Scapa Flow to Russia, and the dead included the British Minister of War, Lord Kitchener. There were only 12 survivors.

5 Betty's Reading Room, Tingwall

HY 402229

Private; open to the public; car park at the pier.

This small croft house has been meticulously restored in memory of local resident Betty Prictor. Inside, a large collection of books may be borrowed, added to, or enjoyed on the comfortable sofas in front of a cosy stove. Local artworks enhance the scene. A quirky library in the most public sense of the word.

6 Ness Battery, Stromness

HY 248079

OIC; tours available, details from Visit Orkney

The Ness Battery saw service in both World Wars. It was built to protect the entrance into Scapa Flow through Hoy Sound, and it included gun houses and observation towers as well as magazines and stores. In 1941 reinforcements were added to protect the gunners from air attacks. Ness Battery is one of the few coastal batteries where wooden accommodation blocks have survived. In the mess hall a remarkable mural depicting the rural landscape may be seen. The site has been recently restored by the Scapa Flow Landscape Partnership and is now open to the public through privately booked tours.

7 Pier Arts Centre, Stromness, Mainland

HY 254091

OIC.

The thriving Pier Arts Centre occupies the old offices, stores and wharf of the Hudsons Bay Company. The building was converted and renovated in 2007, at which time it was recognised with the Royal Incorporation of Architects in Scotland's Andrew Doolan Award for the Best Building in Scotland. Inside it boasts an important collection of modern art including pieces by Barbara Hepworth and many of the St Ives Group, thanks to local benefactor Margaret Gardiner. It also hosts regular exhibitions of local art.

8 Happy Valley, Mainland

HY 327105

OIC; car park off the Bigswell Road.

The steading here is called Bankburn. It was built in the early nineteenth century and was inhabited from 1948 by Edwin Harrold who died in 2005. Mr Harrold wished to create a wooded garden along the banks of the burn and he planted trees and built a network of paths and bridges to enhance the landscape. The house is a good example of a rural dwelling and it has been conserved and renovated by the Scapa Flow Landscape Partnership. The dwelling is not open to the public, but the garden is a popular place to walk.

9 Boat House, Finstown, Mainland

HY 365135

Private.

This is a quirky part of modern Orkney architecture. It was built in the 1970s as part of a complex of holiday chalets. The roof is an old mould for fibreglass boat hulls – a link to the Orkney tradition of using old boats for buildings.

10 Netherbutton, Mainland HY 463044

Private.

Netherbutton was the most northerly station in a chain of radio stations that stretched from Land's End in the 1930s. None of the eight aerial towers are left, but there are various buildings, now converted for other uses. Artefacts relating to the use of the station may be seen in the Orkney Wireless Museum in Kirkwall.

11 Churchill Barriers, HY 483012 – ND 476948
Southern Isles

Spanned by public road, care with traffic needed.

There are four barriers that link Lamb Holm, and the southern chain of islands, to Mainland Orkney. Their original purpose was to create a safe anchorage for the British Fleet within Scapa Flow. This had been attempted in the First World War by the sinking of various ships in the approaches to the Flow, but early in the Second World War a German U-boat, the U47, penetrated the Flow and torpedoed HMS *Royal Oak*; 834 people died. Work on the barriers started with the sinking of rubble, which was not an easy task due to the depth of water and speed of the tide in some places. After this had been accomplished, huge concrete blocks were laid, and eventually the top was capped with a road surface. Over 66,000 blocks, each weighing 5 or 10 tons, had to be cast for the purpose at St Mary's Holm. Much of the labour for this work came from prisoners of war, the scant remains of whose camp may be seen in Lamb Holm. Work on the Barriers was not finished until after the war, and even now they need frequent maintenance.

12 Italian Chapel, Lamb Holm HY 488006

OIC; signposted; car park.

Little remains of the camps used by the prisoners of war who worked on the construction of the Barriers, but rising amidst the concrete foundations of the Lamb Holm camp is a small red and white chapel. This was built by the prisoners themselves, and while the ornate façade and pillared entrance give an idea of what lies inside, they totally belie the materials with which the prisoners had to work.

The chapel is made from two Nissen huts, joined end to end, but inside they are richly and ornately decorated and give little idea of its origin. The walls are painted to resemble carved stonework with brick; cast, moulded concrete has been used for the altar rail, altar and font; and there are elements of wrought iron, including lamps made from recycled beef cans. At the foot of the rood screen gates a small heart has been set into the floor, reputedly in commemoration of a love affair between a local girl and the Italian who wrought the screen. Behind the altar is a large painting of the Madonna and Child based on a painting by Nicolo Barabino, a postcard of which the painter, Domenico Chiocchetti, always kept in his pocket. Many materials used in the construction of the chapel came from the sea.

Chiocchetti had been a church decorator before the war, and he masterminded the building and its decoration. Outside, the position of the camp square is marked by a concrete statue of St George and the Dragon, which is also his work.

The chapel is dedicated to the Queen of Peace. Initially, after the war it began to be badly affected by damp and fell into disrepair, but a return trip by Chiocchetti was organised and he carried out some repairs. It is now better maintained, and one of Orkney's more poignant monuments. More recently, his family made a second return trip and donated some of the mementos of his time working on the chapel.

The chapel is now much visited and well used for concerts, recitals and services.

13 Balfour Battery and Lighthouse, Hoxa Head, South Ronaldsay   ND 403930

Private. A local footpath leads around the site, care needed.

This concrete battery is part of a complex built to protect the main entrance to Scapa Flow. The first modern defences were built here in the First World War, but the present structures date to 1940 when emplacements for twin 6-pounder guns were built together with ammunition magazines and other buildings. The following year the complex was enlarged to add protection from air attack. Nearby stands a cast-iron lighthouse built in 1901 to guide ships into the Flow. It was gas-powered.

14 Buchanan Battery, Flotta ND 373926

Private.

A concrete battery built in 1940 to house twin 6-pounder guns for the defence of the Flow.

15 Oil Terminal, Flotta ND 350940

Private.

Work on the terminal was started in the 1970s, and it is an important site both for Orkney and for Britain. About 10 per cent of the UK's oil output is handled through Flotta and it has provided much employment, though most workers live in Mainland Orkney and commute daily by ferry from Houton. The impact of such industrialisation on a fragile environment has been minimised by the restriction of operations to a single island and by careful construction and landscaping in Flotta. It is likely that oil processing will continue here for some time, but when work does cease the company are committed to reinstatement of the site.

16 Lyness Pumping Station, Hoy ND 309946

OIC; signposted; visitor centre, café and car park.

Lyness was an important naval base during both World Wars. Ships could be maintained and refuelled, and anti-submarine nets laid out and repaired. At the heart of this activity was the Pumping Station and fuel storage area, built in 1917, which used coal-fired (later oil) pumps to bring fuel oil out of the tankers in which it had been transported, and into huge storage tanks. Initially there were four 12,000-ton tanks, in 1936 twelve 15,000-ton tanks were built, and in the 1940s work began to build others in the hillside behind Lyness, though only six were completed. Today, only one tank survives. The remains at Lyness include the harbour piers and concrete ramp for the repair of anti-submarine nets, as well as various sheds and other buildings. During the Second World War Lyness was home to 12,000 personnel and, though it is largely deserted and depleted, many of the buildings survive. Before the construction of the nearby Garrison Theatre, the largest cinema in Europe was sited here. Today, the old Pumping Station has been turned into a visitor centre.

17 Wee Fea Communications Centre   ND 293944

Private.

On the hill above Lyness stands a featureless concrete building. This was the Base HQ and Communications Centre for the naval base at Scapa Flow and it was named HMS *Proserpine*. Over 200 people worked up here. It is not possible to enter the building today, but it is worth visiting for the commanding position and views across the Flow.

18 Garrison Theatre, North Walls, Hoy   ND 307922

Private.

This theatre was built for the troops in the 1940s in typical art-deco style. Behind the façade it was originally based on a huge Nissen hut. After the war it was converted into a private house.

19 Wreck of German Destroyer,   HY 745440
Lopness, Sanday

Just offshore, visible at low tide; car park and picnic table.

The B98 was one of the warships of the German High Seas Fleet that had been interned, and scuttled, in Scapa Flow. Many of these ships, including the B98, were salvaged between the wars. She was being towed south for breaking, but broke loose in a storm and settled on the beach at the north end of Sanday, where she provides an unusual relic of the First World War. The visible remains mainly comprise elements of her turbines and lower hull.

20 Lettan Radar Station and other remains,   HY 758454
Sanday

Private.

Sanday was an important place in the Second World War with installations including two radar stations, a camp and a dummy airfield. Some of the buildings from the Reserve Radar Station at Lettan may still be seen to either side of the road, including a generator house and transmitter blocks. There was a personnel camp to the south of this, of which most buildings have gone, though the long brick-built mortuary building survives, to the east of the road. On the shores of Cata Sand lay a dummy airfield; the operations centre, known as the 'Brickie Hut', stands between the road and the sea at the head of the bay. The plain here could be lit up to resemble an airfield.

21 Bird Observatory, North Ronaldsay   HY 750530

Private.

The North Ronaldsay Bird Observatory was built in 1985, and owes much to the ethos of its times in that it was designed to be energy-efficient, using both solar and wind power. It is also used as a dwelling house and guest house.

Museums

The *Orkney Museum* in Kirkwall is an excellent museum with displays on all aspects of Orkney history and prehistory, including material from many of the individual sites mentioned here. In addition there is a small museum in Stromness that specialises in the natural history and maritime history of the islands and is always interesting to visit. Some of the sites have their own visitor centres: the displays at the *Broch of Gurness* have been updated; there is a fine visitor centre at *Skara Brae*; at *Isbister* there is a small museum made all the more interesting by the opportunity to handle some of the archaeological finds; at *Tormiston Mill* there is a small display relating to Orcadian prehistory in general; the visitor centre at *Orphir* covers Orkney in Norse times; and finally, at *Lyness* on Hoy Orkney Islands Council have set up a visitor centre relating to Scapa Flow in wartime.

There are two museums relating to rural life in more modern times: at *Corrigall Farm* and *Kirbuster Farm* in Mainland Orkney. These are both good places to visit, with plenty of interesting information and activities often taking place to demonstrate the traditional tasks and routines of daily life in the eighteenth and nineteenth centuries.

In addition, there are a number of private museums and visitor centres that cover many aspects of the human and natural heritage of Orkney. Information about their whereabouts, and opening hours, may be obtained from Visit Orkney.

Finally, heritage centres and displays exist in most of the Outer Isles; information may be obtained from individual websites and Visit Orkney.

The Ranger service provided by Historic Scotland for the World Heritage Sites offers an excellent programme of walks and events (www.orkneycommunities.co.uk/ORKNEYRANGERS/), and there are Rangers on several of the other islands.

Further Reading

Leaflets and Guidebooks

Individual site leaflets and guidebooks are currently available with information about the following monuments: the Bishop's Palace in Kirkwall; the Brough of Birsay; Dounby Click Mill; the Earl's Palace in Kirkwall; Gurness; Isbister, Maeshowe; Noltland Castle; Skara Brae; and St Magnus Cathedral. Most of these are produced by Historic Scotland and they are widely available throughout the islands. In addition, leaflets about other sites and related topics are frequently produced and updated by Orkney Islands Council and by various private individuals and organisations. Visit Orkney is a good source of information on current material, as are the Orkney Museum and Kirkwall Public Library.

There is a wide range of books available on Orkney archaeology and history. The following is a guide to some of the key texts. Excellent bookshops are to be found in both Kirkwall and Stromness.

Books and Articles

Anderson P. *The Stewart Earls of Orkney* (Edinburgh: John Donald 2012).

Ashmore, P. J., *Neolithic and Bronze Age Scotland* (London: Historic Scotland and BT Batsford 1996).

Ballin-Smith, B., *Howe, four millennia of Orkney prehistory* (Edinburgh: Society of Antiquaries of Scotland, monograph series, 9, 1994).

Barry, G., *History of the Orkney Islands* (Edinburgh: Constable 1805; reprinted by Mercat Press 1975).

Berry, R. J., *The Natural History of Orkney* (London: Collins, The New Naturalist Library 1985).

Berry, R. J. and Firth, H. N. (eds), *The People of Orkney* (Kirkwall: The Orkney Press, Aspects of Orkney 4, 1986).

Booth, C., Cuthbert, M., and Reynolds, P., *The Birds of Orkney* (Kirkwall: The Orkney Press 1984).

Bullard, E., *Wildflowers in Orkney, a new checklist* (Kirkwall: privately published 1995).

Burgher, L., *Orkney, an illustrated architectural guide* (Edinburgh: Royal Incorporation of Architects in Scotland 1991).

Crawford, B., *Scandinavian Scotland* (Leicester: Leicester University Press 1987).

Davidson, J. L. and Henshall, A. S., *The Chambered Tombs of Orkney* (Edinburgh: Edinburgh University Press 1989).

Dean, T. and Hall, T. *The Orkney Book of Birds* (Kirkwall: *The Orcadian* 2008).

Donaldson, G., *A Northern Commonwealth: Scotland and Norway* (Edinburgh: Saltire Society 1990).

Downes, J., Foster, S. and Wickham-Jones, C.R. with Callister, J. (eds) *The Heart of Neolithic Orkney World Heritage Site, Research Agenda* (Edinburgh: Historic Scotland 2005). (This document, and updates, may be freely downloaded from the Historic Scotland website.)

Downes, J. & Ritchie, A. *Sea Change: Orkney and Northern Europe in the Late Iron Age AD 300-800* (Angus: Pinkfoot Press 2003).

Fenton, A., *The Northern Isles: Orkney and Shetland* (Edinburgh: John Donald 1978).

Fitzpatrick, A. P., 'The submission of the Orkney Isles to Claudius: new evidence?' (Scottish Archaeological Review 6, 24–34, 1989).

Foster, S. M., 'Transformation in social space: the Iron Age of Orkney and Caithness' (Scottish Archaeological Review 6, 34–55, 1989).

Foster, S. M., *Picts, Gaels and Scots* (London: Historic Scotland and BT Batsford 1996).

Garnham, T. *Lines on the Landscape, Circles from the Sky* (Gloucester: Tempus 2004).

Gifford, J., *The Buildings of Scotland: Highlands and Islands* (London: Penguin Books 1992).

Gunn, J., *The Orkney Book* (London: Thomas Nelson & Sons Ltd 1909).

Hedges, J. W., *Tomb of the Eagles, a window on Stone Age tribal Britain* (London: John Murray Ltd 1984).

Historic Scotland, *Monuments of Orkney* (Edinburgh: Historic Scotland 2012)

Hjaltalin, H. J. and Goudie, G. (trans), *The Orkneyinga Saga* (Edinburgh: Mercat Press 1977).

Hunter, J. R., 'A new neolithic burial cairn in Orkney?' (*Proc Soc Antiq Scot* 123, 9–12, 1993).

Linklater, E., *Orkney and Shetland* (London: Robert Hale Ltd 1965).

Low, G., *Orkney and Schetland 1774* (Inverness: Melven Press).

Marwick, H., *Orkney* (London: Robert Hale Ltd 1951).

Marwick, H., *Orkney Farm Names* (Kirkwall 1952).

Muir, T., *The Shorter Orkneyinga Saga* (Kirkwall, Orkney Museums and Heritage 2006).

Muir, T., (ed) *Orkney in the Sagas* (Kirkwall: Orkney Museums and Heritage 2006).

Muir, T., *Landscapes of Scapa Flow* (Kirkwall: *The Orcadian*, 2013)

Nicolaisen, W. F. H., *Scottish Place-names* (London: BT Batsford 1976).

Owen, O. (ed), *The World of Orkneyinga Saga* (Kirkwall: Orkney Museums and Heritage 2006).

Paris, P. *Orkney's Italian Chapel* (Edinburgh: Black & White Publishing 2013)

Renfrew, C. (ed), *The Prehistory of Orkney* (Edinburgh: Edinburgh University Press 1985).

Ritchie, A., *Exploring Scotland's Heritage: Orkney and Shetland* (Edinburgh: The Stationery Office 1985).

Ritchie, A. (ed), *Neolithic Orkney in its European Context* (Cambridge: MacDonald Institute Monographs 2000).

Royal Commission on the Ancient and Historical Monuments of Scotland, *An Inventory of the Ancient and Historical Monuments of Orkney and Shetland* (Edinburgh: Her Majesty's Stationery Office 1946).

Schei, L. K. and Moberg, G., *The Orkney Story* (London: BT Batsford 1985).

Schrank, G., *An Orkney Estate, improvements at Graemeshall 1827–88* (Phantassie, East Linton: Tuckwell Press 1995).

Scott, Sir Walter, *The Pirate* (Edinburgh: Constable 1821).

Shearer, J., Groundwater, W. and Mackay, J. D., *The New Orkney Book* (London: Thomas Nelson & Sons Ltd 1966).

Sharples, N. M., 'Excavations at Pierowall Quarry, Westray, Orkney' (Edinburgh: *Proc Soc Antiq Scot* 114, 75–125, 1984).

Tait, C., *The Orkney Guide Book* (Orkney: Charles Tait Photographic 2012).

Thomson, W. P. L., *Kelp-making in Orkney* (Kirkwall: The Orkney Press 1983).

Thomson, W. P. L., *The New History of Orkney* (Kirkwall: *The Orcadian* 2012).

Tudor, J., *The Orkneys and Shetland: their past and present state* (London: Edward Stanford 1883).

Wickham-Jones, C.R., *Between the Wind and the Water: World Heritage Orkney* (Oxford: Oxbow Books 2006).

Index